MPORTANCE TO NATURE

By Dan Dagget

with photography by Tom Bean

ACKNOWLEDGMENTS

First and foremost, I would like to thank Mark and Rachel Thatcher and their son Ishai of the Thatcher Charitable Trust whose generous support made this book possible. Mark's name will be familiar to many of you as the inventor of the sport sandal and founder of Teva Sandals. Mark has a deep and abiding commitment to the environment, born, no doubt, on his many trips down the Colorado River as a Grand Canyon river guide. Rachel is equally as concerned, committed, and involved. Interestingly, as Mark, Rachel, and I were discussing the progress of the book after I had already decided to name it *Gardeners of Eden*, Mark told me something very interesting about the meaning of the word *teva*. He said that a rabbinical scholar with whom he had discussed the word in depth had told him that, in ancient Hebrew, *teva* referred to a "stamp" that could impose order on an amorphous medium—sealing wax, for instance. From that, the scholar said, the word came to refer to the order God imposed onto chaos to create the world and, ultimately, nature (which is why Mark used Teva as his company's trademark). The scholar continued that, in this same way, *teva* also refers to the result of the first use of God's stamp on the world—the Garden of Eden. I guess Teva was meant to sponsor this book.

Also responsible for the creation of this book are the people who created the examples of outstanding stewardship that inspired me to write it and provided the material to fill it. Included among these exceptional individuals are land stewards, scientists, government staffers, activists, and people who are just plain concerned about the environment. Of those, I stand most in awe of the stewards who shaped the land directly. They work harder than many of us would ever think of working, pursuing goals the rest of us consider impossible. Most of them could make a lot more money doing something else, but they don't, and the rest of us benefit from it.

Credit is due as well to the foundations and other entities that contributed support which made many of the examples described in these pages possible. Among those are the Collective Heritage Institute (which holds the annual Bioneers conference in Marin, California), the Arizona Department of Environmental Quality, the National Fish and Wildlife Foundation, and the San Francisco Foundation.

I would like to thank Tom Bean for taking the wonderful photographs you'll find here and for accompanying me on many of my travels. Tom makes a great conversationalist and is a good person to have around during an interview. He asked a number of questions I probably would have never thought of. While I'm at it, I'd like to thank Gary Nabhan and Courtney White for reading the manuscript and offering suggestions on how to make it more effective.

A number of people contributed to this book who aren't mentioned within its pages. Most of you know who you are, and to you I say, "Thank you," and "I apologize." I know how frustrating it can be not to be mentioned in something written about your work and your passion.

Last, but not least, I'd like to thank you for choosing this book and reading at least this far.

This book is published by
The Thatcher Charitable Trust
Contact in care of EcoResults!
P. O. Box 61613
Santa Barbara, CA 93160

Book designers: cover, Larry Lindahl; book design, Jane Perini.
Photography © 2004 by Tom Bean (unless otherwise noted).
Printed in Canada

Library of Congress Control Number: 2005903089

Dan Dagget
Gardeners of Eden: Rediscovering Our Importance to Nature
Written by Dan Dagget
Photographs by Tom Bean
ISBN 0-9666229-1-X

1. environmental issues, public land management, humans and nature, endangered species, preservation and conservation, ranching, range management, ecology, range ecology, grazing, wilderness, native species, ecosystem restoration, restoration ecology, livestock management.

CONTENTS

"There is a way that nature speaks,

that land speaks. Most of the time we are

simply not patient enough, quiet enough,

to pay attention to the story."

– LINDA HOGAN, CHICKASAW WRITER AND POET

Parkland rangeland near Hollister, California

− INTRODUCTION −

YOU CAN'T HAVE YOUR CAKE UNLESS YOU EAT IT, TOO

ON DUEL-ISM ■ LIVING LIKE BEES, BEAVERS, AND WOLVES
USING ALIEN SOLUTIONS TO EARTHLY PROBLEMS
BECOMING NATIVE AGAIN

The argument over how we should live in relation to the rural and remote lands of the American West hasn't changed much in more than a century. John Muir, founder of the Sierra Club and father of the modern environmental movement, said in the late nineteenth century that we should reduce our impact on those lands as much as possible and preserve and protect all that we can. Most certainly, Muir and his followers insist, we should protect as much as possible of that which has remained relatively untainted by human alteration—the wilderness, the wildlands.

Others have maintained, on the other hand, that it is our right to use whatever we choose because God created it for us or merely because there is no good reason not to. Still others, the middle-of-the-roaders, say, "It would be nice if we could protect everything, but we've got to be realists…" They concede the high road to the preservationists but turn the dispute into a struggle of idealism versus realism, the moral versus the practical, small-is-beautiful versus more-is-better.

This fits right into our duelistic society of liberals versus conservatives, Republicans versus Democrats, and tree-huggers versus wise-users, and plays to our prejudice that the solution to all environmental problems is "victory for our side." Within this us-versus-them scenario, a few try to achieve compromise or find a middle ground, but no one, or almost no one, asks if these are really the only two alternatives.

They aren't. There is another alternative, one that is much less divisive and much more hopeful. There is a way to enrich the land as we use it; a way we can benefit the plants,

3

animals, and ecosystems with which we share this planet as we benefit ourselves.

If this sounds too good to be true, or too close to violating the maxim that "you can't have your cake and eat it, too," the message detailed within this book is more radical than that. The message you'll read here is "you can't have your cake *unless* you eat it, too."

This is not news. Bees, beavers, wolves, and more plants and animals than there is time or room to list have been operating under this maxim for millennia. Bees pollinate flowers as they consume nectar and, in the process, create more plants and more flowers and, therefore, more food for more bees. Beavers eat willows and use them to construct dams which create ponds and enlarge meadows. That creates more habitat for more willows and more beavers. Wolves cull the sick and slow among the deer, keeping the herds genetically healthy so they prosper and continue to feed more wolves.

Until recently (for the first 99 percent of our existence), humans fit into nature in this same mutually beneficial way. As hunters and gatherers, as pastoralists, and even as small-scale farmers and gardeners, we benefited the ecosystems of which we were a part in much the way beavers, bees, and wolves do. Some of us still live in this naturally interdependent way.

A much larger and faster-growing percentage of us, however, get our food, fiber, and other products from nature via a system of extractive technologies more characteristic of aliens than of a mutually interdependent community of natives. We have developed this extractive technology for good reason, of course—it produces food, fiber, and other things we need in prodigious amounts, insulating us from the effects of drought and the other vagaries

For most of our existence, humans have benefited ecosystems by serving as hunters and gatherers, pastoralists, and small-scale farmers. These herders in Kazakhstan still do.

PHOTO: DAVE EDWARD

of less-technological agriculture. But living as an alien has its downside, too. It threatens the breakdown of important ecological functions via global warming and the endangering of species. It erodes the connection between humans and nature as we turn our communities into a series of urban and suburban space stations surrounded by an "exploitosphere" from which we extract everything from food to recreation.

Some of us have become aware of the downside our alienation creates and have begun to try various means to counter it. Ironically, those countermeasures have been, for the most part, just as alien as the situation they were created to correct. Rather than restoring our old relationships with the ecos of which we were once an important part, these countermeasures have removed us even further from it. To try to counter the effects of our alien technology, we have created ever-larger preserves and protected areas, and removed ourselves and our impacts from them. Acting as if we're trying to fool nature into thinking that we're not here, we have behaved as aliens would. We treat this land outside our exploitosphere as if it were a combination art exhibit, zoo, cathedral, and adventure park. There we limit ourselves to roles as sightseers, worshipers, caretakers, and joyriders. Exacerbating the situation, we make our technological system ever-more extractive, efficient, and detached in the mistaken belief that the way to heal the damage we do is to create less connection rather than more.

The problem with all this is that we humans were once a part, in some cases a very important part, of the very ecosystems we're trying to restore by removing ourselves from them. This dooms us to trying to put back together an extremely complex puzzle with a very important piece missing—us. And, when we discover that this alien-style solution doesn't work, we don't relent, we just do it harder. We remove ourselves from ever-larger pieces of nature (or at least we pretend to), and we create more and more stringent limits on our involvement in those areas from which we can't remove ourselves.

And as we do all of this, we neglect the obvious truth that, if removing wolves or some other predator does harm to an ecosystem, if causing a species such as the red-legged frog or the tiger salamander to become extinct threatens the security of all other species, as some of us claim, then it stands to reason that removing humans who have played a more widespread, more impactive role must cause even greater problems.

In spite of this, hardly anyone, to my knowledge, is expressing concern about the removal of humans from the roles within the ecosystem that we have evolved to play, and that Nature has evolved to have us play. Nor is anyone conducting studies to determine what those roles were or what changes have occurred because we no longer fulfill them. Most important, perhaps, no one is trying to reintroduce humans into the environment to have us resume our duties as hunters, herders, gatherers, and whatever else, even though we're going to great ends to restore animals that have played much less significant roles.

A much larger and faster-growing percentage of us, however, get our food, fiber, and other products from nature via a system of extractive technologies more characteristic of aliens than of a mutually interdependent community of natives.

Sometimes I wonder what Earth's ecosystems think has happened to the two-leggeds who once served them so well. Where did those beings go who once played such an important role as predators, foragers, and cultivators? Have they vanished? Been abducted? Gone extinct? And then I wonder what those same ecosystems think of this new being which walks in their midst, which resembles the one that has disappeared in every way except that the new one keeps none of the old responsibilities, the old agreements. Is it an impostor? An alien body-snatcher who has removed the old ones and taken their place? In a way, it is. Or rather, we are.

In fact, most of us know about as much about restoring a Martian ecosystem as we do an earthly one.

This book offers an alternative to living on Earth as aliens. It offers a way to become native once again, to reassume some of the responsibilities we evolved to uphold, at least as much as is possible in the context of a modern technological world. The stories that follow are about reintroducing humans into the environment in the same way that we might reintroduce an endangered subspecies of caribou or flycatcher or cactus. They make the point that this is as important in the case of humans as it is in the case of those other living things, and for the same reason—because, as we remove ourselves from those old mutualisms by acting as aliens, we leave as big a hole, if not a bigger one, than those other life forms have left.

That may set off your alarms in a couple of ways. "Ecosystems got along just fine before there were humans!" you may say. Or you might ask, "How could it be possible that humans are abandoning the planet when there are so many of us, and it's so obvious that we're overwhelming it?"

As for the first of those questions, it's true that the earthly community got along fine before there were humans, just as it got along fine before there were bees and beavers and plenty of other things. But those pre-human communities were made up of different species than the one we evolved to be a part of. Those old communities and many of the species that comprised them are gone. The community of which humans evolved to be an important part is still here.

As for how I could say that humans are abandoning the planet while it seems so obvious that we are overrunning it, that brings us back to the alien/native distinction. It's the people who are living as aliens who are overrunning the planet. Those who are living as natives are few and getting fewer. Some remain as holdouts from traditional ways of being. Others are the products of their own do-it-yourself reintroduction program. Examples of both are the subject of this book.

Last, but not least, others have expressed concern that the claim that humans have been an essential part of nature, and can once again become so, is just a restatement of the old arrogance that our species has been granted dominion over nature. This arrogance, critics say, has been used to excuse all sorts of environmental profligacies. Humans have certainly done things to harm the environment, and the claim that we have dominion over nature has certainly been used as a means to excuse such harms, but the examples that follow in this book are not examples of domination; they are examples of mutualism and synergy. And while it may be accurate to level the charge of arrogance when humans are blinded by

Sometimes I wonder what Earth's ecosystems think has happened to the two-leggeds who once served them so well. Where did those beings go who once played such an important role as predators, foragers, and cultivators? Have they vanished? Been abducted? Gone extinct?

our claims of domination and do harm, that charge makes no sense when it is directed at humans playing roles we have evolved to play and that nature relies on us to play. We don't call beavers arrogant when they create ponds that water meadows that grow cottonwoods that feed more beavers. Nor do we call bees greedy or exploitative when they consume nectar while they pollinate flowers to make more flowers to support more bees.

The purpose of this book is to dispel smoke rather than to create it. One way in which it achieves this purpose is by revealing an environmental smokescreen of which most of us are unaware, and behind which a whole class of environmental wrongs goes undetected. It also clears our environmental view by showing us how to restore feedback loops between humans and nature that have shriveled and ceased to function as a result of our adoption of an alien agriculture and a just-as-alien environmentalism.

Why should you listen to what I have to say about these things? I'm not a scientist, but I have been an environmental activist for thirty-one years. I started my activist journey fighting coal strip mines in southeastern Ohio. From there I moved west to Arizona where I worked to designate remote public lands as wilderness, fought to tighten the restrictions that governed what ranchers could do to protect their livestock from mountain lions and black bears, and helped initiate a campaign to ban uranium mining in the vicinity of the Grand Canyon. My involvement in that latter campaign included helping to put together some of the first demonstrations organized by Earth First!, one of the most radical of environmental groups. During this part of my environmental career, I was designated one of the 100 top grass-roots activists in the United States by the Sierra Club (in 1992).

More recently, I have been involved in putting together a collaborative conflict-resolution group involving ranchers and environmentalists that has been used as a model for other groups. I wrote a Pulitzer Prize-nominated book (*Beyond the Rangeland Conflict: Toward a West That Works*) about this experience and have been called on to give well over a hundred presentations about it around the West. Lately, I created an environmental organization named EcoResults! that secures grants to fund efforts by rural people to restore damaged lands and bring them back to environmental function. As part of my involvement in EcoResults! I've done my share of spreading seed and mulch, piling rocks in gullies, reading monitoring transects, and acting like a predator by herding animals.

My methods, in other words, have changed, but my values haven't. I still value open country, wild land, wildlife, predators, and healthy ecosystems as much as I ever did, maybe more. Now, however, instead of trying to serve those values by demonstration, regulation, and litigation, I work with people who live on the land and ask it what it needs and respond when it answers. ■

The purpose of this book is to dispel smoke rather than to create it. One way in which it achieves this purpose is by revealing an environmental smokescreen of which most of us are unaware, and behind which a whole class of environmental wrongs goes undetected.

CHAPTER ONE

PINK PANTHERS AND LOST TRIBES

RESTORING LIFE TO DEAD LAND ▪ THE PINK PANTHER PEOPLE
A LOST TRIBE AMONG US ▪ SHOWING DOG TRICKS
TO CAT FANATICS ▪ THE LEAVE-IT-ALONE ASSUMPTION
MAKING THE ENVIRONMENT IRRELEVANT ▪ A SCANDAL IN EDEN

In the central Nevada desert, near the tiny almost-ghost town of Mina, lives a couple who are the most effective restorers of ecosystems I have been able to locate in more than twenty years of searching. This man and woman can take land that is as close to biologically dead as land gets, and they can return it to a state of health, vitality, and diversity that most of us would call miraculous. They can do this with land that has been rendered ecologically comatose by abuse, overuse, pollution, neglect, or whatever, and they can restore it to the point that it blooms with grasses and shrubs and is reinhabited by birds, lizards, deer, bugs, and all manner of critters. Even more impressively, they can do this in the most difficult of conditions—in the high desert of Nevada where ten inches of rain in a year is a "wet spell," and three inches is more usual.

For some time now, I have been amazed by what these people, Tony and Jerrie Tipton, can do. In fact, they were the topic of the last chapter of my first book, *Beyond the Rangeland Conflict: Toward a West That Works*, which was published just before the calendar changed to 1996. They helped bring that book to a conclusion by doing something extraordinary— by bringing back to life a piece of devastated land that had been denuded by a mining operation. I've chosen to have them help kick off this book because they have surpassed that earlier achievement with another even more amazing.

The Tiptons and their continuing story provide a thread of continuity that helps establish that the land-restoration methods described in that book remain effective over time. (but you don't have to read the first book to "get it"). In the same way the first book supports the stories in this one, indicating that the successes described here aren't going to bloom and fade in a year or two.

Getting back to that "surpassing achievement"—a scientist who went to see for himself told me, "If they [the Tiptons] had come to me and said they thought they could do something like this, I wouldn't have bothered to laugh at them. I would have thought they were too crazy to laugh at. But they did it, and I've seen it, and it's still there [three years after completion]."

The eco disaster the Tiptons tackled was a three-hundred-foot-high pile of crushed rock called a heap-leach pad. This pile consisted of low-quality gold ore extracted from a pit, crushed to rocks fist-size or smaller, and piled on a huge sheet of sloped, foot-thick black plastic with a collection basin at the bottom. A solution containing cyanide was then sprayed on the pile to trickle down through the rocky ore and dissolve the minute amounts of gold it contained. The pile was sprayed with this solution for several years, until the gold dwindled to amounts too small to make the operation profitable. At that point, the company sprayed water on the pile to wash out the cyanide. This was done in order to make the pile capable of growing enough plants so that the mining company could say it had "reclaimed" the heap and avoid forfeiting the guarantee it had posted with the government in order to be permitted to mine the area.

There was no soil. In fact, there were hardly any of the fine particles of rock that are the raw material for soil. Adding to the difficulty, the pile had literally been sterilized by a lethal substance—cyanide.

To give you an idea of the magnitude of the challenge that cyanide-leached pile of rock presented to anyone who would try to grow plants on it: there was no soil. In fact, there were hardly any of the fine particles of rock that are the raw material for soil. Adding to the difficulty, the pile had literally been sterilized by a lethal substance—cyanide. This made it even more inhospitable to plants, most of which require some organic material in the soil in order to grow. The most serious problem, however, came from all the water, with and without cyanide, that had been sprayed on the pile for years. In Nevada's dry climate, a portion of every drop of that highly mineralized water had evaporated, leaving behind the mineral salts it contained. This covered the cyanide-sterilized rock pile with a crust of salt that made it almost impossible for plants to grow there. Something called the salt absorption rate (SAR) is a measure of the amount of salt that plants have to tolerate in order to live in a place. The SAR on that pile of rocks was 200. To receive bond release, that quantity would have to be lowered to less than 10.

The mining company had tried to reclaim this toxic rock pile with the best methods and machinery modern technology had to offer. Using a device called a hydroseeder, they had sprayed it with a mixture of seeds, fertilizer, and a plasticized mulch (the same sort of stuff highway departments spray onto road-construction sites), and then they had irrigated it. After all this effort, the only thing that grew in any abundance was a nonnative annual weed named halogeton. Halogeton is poisonous to many creatures that would try to eat it. Because these plants are annuals, they died after one season. The desert wind blew away what was left of them, and the company was back to where it started.

When the Tiptons asked for a chance to try their technique on the pile, to prove they could do better than technology, the mining company figured it had little to lose. After thinking the matter over, it granted them permission.

The tools with which the Tiptons dared to tackle this area, where the best of technology had just failed, would have convinced most of us they were crazy. The tools they chose could hardly be simpler—native plant seeds, hay and straw (to add organic matter to an environment that had none), a few experienced trucks, and cows. Yes, cows.

First, the Tiptons dragged a length of railroad rail over the part of the pile they intended to treat, breaking up the salt crust. The rail also served the purpose of knocking the sharp points off the rocks so they wouldn't make the cows footsore. Then they scattered the seed, spread the hay and straw, and released the cattle. The cows ate most of the hay and a little of the straw, and what they didn't eat, they trampled into the rocks along with the seeds and the microbe-rich organic fertilizer they provided from their guts. After a few short days of this treatment, the Tiptons removed the animals and let the mixture gestate.

Six months later, a community of native plants had grown where the Tiptons had conducted their trial. More amazing than that, the salt absorption rate on the treated part of the pile had been reduced to 3.6, well below the target of 10 required for bond release, and well within the limits considered necessary for plants to germinate and survive. The only explanation available was that the organic waste the animals had processed and injected into the rocks had created a soil microbial community that transformed the area.

Three years after the treatment, the scientist I quoted a few paragraphs back—Al Medina of the Rocky Mountain Research Station of the U.S. Forest Service—visited the site. He found that it was not only still supporting the native plants, but that a diverse community of wildlife was using it as well. Medina took photos of birds' nests, rodent burrows, coyote and deer dung, and a number of lizards.

I interviewed Medina about the project a couple of years after that visit, and he made the statement that I quoted earlier. But he added something else that takes this project from the realm of unlikely to the level of the truly incredible.

"The Tiptons did lie to me about something very important about this project," Medina said. "They told me they achieved all of this on only one inch of precipitation [that's how much the Tiptons said had fallen during the time the trial was conducted]. I checked. They only got nine-tenths."

PHOTOS: DAN DAGGET

Top: The heap-leach pad—300 feet of crushed rock leached with cyanide and encrusted with salt. Bottom: Four years after restoration by the Tiptons—the rock pile supports a community of native plants and animals.

When I visited the site five years after the Tiptons' trial, the plants, lizards, and birds were still there, and fresh coyote and deer dung indicated those animals were still using the area as well. On the rest of the heap-leach pad, which had been reclaimed by technological means and irrigated, there was still little more than weeds.

The Tiptons had grown a healthy community of native plants on a pile of rocks polluted with cyanide and covered with salt on less than an inch of precipitation. We usually associate such out-of-the-ordinary successes with massive infusions of technology—fertilizer, genetically modified seeds, irrigation—as well as piles of money, but the Tiptons achieved their success using no more technology than the vehicles necessary to haul materials to the site. Even more notable, while they were restoring this piece of devastated land they were creating a useful, harvestable product—food. In fact, in a significant way, it was their producing food that caused the healing.

Tony and Jerrie Tipton—these most effective ecosystem restorers live in a run-down, purple Greyhound-style bus converted to an RV.

Think of what this might mean for poor rural communities around the world. How many of them have land nearby that is ecologically damaged? In many cases, living in ecologically degraded areas is what keeps them poor. How many of them have the tools that I have just named—seeds, at least a little hay and organic waste for mulch, animals, and elbow grease. Poor rural communities could use this technique to heal the land on which they rely for sustenance. It could provide them with the only means proved effective to reduce a runaway birthrate and attendant population explosion—prosperity.

Every year Americans send billions of dol-lars to groups that don't achieve results even remotely comparable to what the Tiptons have achieved and continue to achieve. Here they inspect a riparian area recovery with members of the Western Shoshone Tribe and the U.S. Bureau of Land Management.

At this point you're probably wondering why you haven't heard of these two eco-restorationists. And you're probably thinking they must be very much in demand, unbelievably busy, terribly overworked, and paid very, very well for what they do. Universities, governments, the U.N. must be ringing their phone off the hook trying to sign them up to hold seminars and workshops and conduct restorations.

If this is what you're thinking, you have good reason, because in the world in which we live, there is much work for people with such a skill to do. There are plenty of places that are desertified, denuded, depleted of wildlife and biodiversity; places that our best efforts and most powerful technologies have been unable to heal for years, and in some cases, for centuries.

The Tiptons should be highly respected and wealthy because of it, but they're not. Instead of enjoying the success of, say, a midlevel environmental lawyer or an executive of a run-of-the-mill not-for-profit organization, i.e., living in a $300,000+ house and driving a new SUV, these most effective ecosystem restorers live in a run-down, purple Greyhound-style bus converted to an RV. The bus is rusting and faded. Its tires are cracked from the sun. And on its rear end a previous owner painted a pink panther that peeks back between its legs, mooning whoever follows. One of the last times I saw this fading piece of kitsch it was parked in the middle of a scrap yard surrounded by various kinds of rusting mining equipment—evidence of the job the Tiptons have had to take up to make ends meet—mine salvage. Among the clutter of dismantled conveyer systems and skeletons of metal buildings was a repair shed with a huge door leading to a grease pit in its interior. Large winches hung from its ceiling, providing a means to transform equipment once used for mining into tools for restoring rangeland.

The Tiptons should be prosperous because every year Americans send billions of dollars to groups that promise to make the land more healthy yet don't achieve results even remotely comparable to what these two mavericks have achieved and continue to achieve. Every year surveys tell us that environmental degradation is one of the prime concerns of people around the world, and that many of those people would gladly "pay a little more" to support environmental healing. In spite of this, Tony and Jerrie, the people of the Pink Panther, continue to spend their own money, sweat, equipment, creativity, and limited life-spans tackling ever-more difficult projects in ever-more difficult conditions. They work like prospectors trying to make a strike on the mother lode of acceptance by tackling and subduing problems so impossible, so undoable that they hope the rest of us get the point that what they do actually works. They work harder than most of us would ever consider working, and they continue to succeed, and they continue to live in the Pink Panther and salvage abandoned mine equipment to replenish their grubstake.

The more I became aware of this astonishing discrepancy between what is and what ought to be, the more I was convinced that it had to reveal something substantial about the way our society works, or rather the way it doesn't work, at least with regard to environmental matters.

The more I became aware of this astonishing discrepancy between what is and what ought to be, the more I was convinced that it had to reveal something substantial about the way our society works, or rather the way it doesn't work, at least with regard to environmental matters.

First I had to consider, though, that there might be a perfectly good explanation for all this. The Tiptons could be phonies. Their successes could be clever fakes, fortunate accidents, or even just wishful thinking backed up by bad (or dishonest) monitoring. But the Pink Panther is filled to overflowing with monitoring data and "before and after" photos proving this is anything but a fake. The Tiptons have jaw-dropping examples, lots of them, and they'll take anyone interested enough out on the land to see these in person to prove what they do is no fluke. They'll take you, too, if you show up when they have the time. And they will show you their failures as well as their successes.

You could say that perhaps no one's beating a path to the Tiptons' door because no one knows about them, and you could provide the fact that you've never heard of them as evidence of that. But Tony and Jerrie have given presentations to dozens of forums, to a Secretary of the Interior, to congressmen, to senators, to government land managers, to college professors, to investors, and to audiences that have included leaders of environmental groups. Articles have been written about them. I included their story in a book I wrote that has sold out three printings and is on its way to selling out a fourth.

The methods they use could be too artificial or too intrusive for the environmentally concerned among us to support. That would at least explain why environmentalists haven't flocked to their techniques. But the tools they use are all natural and organic enough to be bought at your local organic-gardening store. They're more natural and low-tech than what most environmental groups use to do their restorations.

It could be the case that these problems are already being solved by conventional means, so there's no reason to solve them with animals and hay and hard work. But the people of the Pink Panther intentionally tackle challenges for which technology and conventional thinking have failed—in some cases several times—and they have succeeded, in spades.

Last of all, you could say that the Tiptons may just be an anomaly. Maybe they truly can do what they do, but no one else can—like a high-wire walker. In that case they would qualify as a curiosity but nothing more. But that's not true either. Others, hundreds, maybe thousands, have used the same methods the Tiptons use, and while most haven't created successes of the same magnitude as the Tiptons, some have. In Arizona, at about the same time the Tiptons did their first restoration in 1989, a man named Terry Wheeler used similar methods to get grass to grow on a thousand-plus-acre pile of copper-mine tailings. Technology had failed on that tailings pile, too. Fifteen years later the grass that Wheeler got to grow is still there, and although most of the mines in Arizona now use some form of the reclamation technique he developed, the technique has not truly been accepted by the mining community.

These other successful restorationists may not live in a rusting RV like the Tiptons, but they do live in a similar state of exile and disregard. They're like a lost tribe dispersed among us whose members possess an important skill that could be extremely valuable to the rest of us if we would bother to ask and to listen, but we don't. We don't listen because we consider the members of this "tribe" to be irrelevant, out of date, out of fashion, weird, crude, obsessed. That's not a lot different than other lost tribes—indigenous peoples scattered and neglected, whose skills and knowledge are considered to be little more than curiosities in our cocksure technological society.

When I realized what had been achieved by the Tiptons, Terry Wheeler, and other members of the Lost Tribe those pioneers comprised, I was blown away. I was so impressed that, after I completed my first book, I continued to follow the efforts of some of them—visiting, photographing, monitoring. And I began to travel the West showing a collection of photos of the most incredible of their successes to anybody who would take the time to look. I made a special point of taking this information to my environmentalist peers. I showed them the cyanide rock pile example, and the mine tailings example. I also showed them instances in which the same technique the Tiptons had used to restore that heap-leach pad had been used to bring life back to areas of desertified rangeland. On some of these areas, the living upper layer of the soil in which most life exists had been washed away, and the subsoil layers were washing away, and the few plants that remained were toppling into rapidly growing gullies.

In many cases, the response to my presentations was positive. Members of an activist vegetarian group wondered how they could support these good stewards without buying the steaks they produced. A member of another group who saw my slide show and then visited some of those same projects firsthand wrote back to the conference organizer: "You not only changed my mind, you changed my life." As I write this, I've done nearly two hundred presentations, from Fargo to Santa Barbara, and the response has been overwhelmingly positive.

But in the cases where my presentation could really have changed things—in presentations to people who work for or lead the groups that receive most of those billions that we spend on environmental issues—I have been treated as a member of the Lost Tribe myself. In all but a very few cases, when I showed those environmental leaders photos of what the methods used by the Tiptons could achieve, there was not a flicker of interest. It was as if I were showing pictures of dog tricks to a bunch of cat fanatics.

When I showed those environmental leaders photos of what the methods used by the Tiptons could achieve, there was not a flicker of interest. It was as if I were showing pictures of dog tricks to a bunch of cat fanatics.

This was true even when the people to whom I was making my presentation were involved in "saving" or "protecting" lands where similar problems were epidemic. Though they were faced with similar problems and were able to do little if anything about them, not one ever expressed any interest in trying the Lost Tribe's method to see if it would work in their case.

I want to make it clear here that what I was showing these people was not chump change. Not only were these successes impressive solutions to serious problems, but they were solutions that were achieved in almost every case by people that we normally think of as being at odds with one another (ranchers and environmentalists, vegetarians and meat producers). That matter alone, in my opinion, should have piqued my listeners' interest. In a world filled with confrontation and conflict, it would seem that a method that solves

What I was showing these people was not chump change but impressive solutions to serious problems. Included were the mine restoration pictured above and below left, and the revitalized riparian area below right.

PHOTOS TOP AND ABOVE LEFT: COURTESY OF THE TIPTONS   PHOTO: DAN DAGGET

problems by bringing people together rather than by pitting them against one another should not have been passed over lightly.

On some occasions, I would press the case, especially when I knew the person I was talking to was familiar with what I was talking about.

I pressed especially hard with one individual whom I knew had seen some of these solutions in person. Before he got a job with a regional environmental group, he had even participated in a collaborative management group with people who used some of these same techniques. I asked him if there was some really tough problem his group was struggling with on which they might be interested in trying the Lost Tribe's method to see if it would work.

"I'd like to help," he said, "but lately I've become more interested in the idea of self-willed land, of what the land can become if we leave it alone. I believe that's the only way we can truly heal the damage we've caused."

This, of course, is the essence of contemporary environmentalism—this assumption that the only way we can really heal the land is to protect it from impacts created by humans: to "leave it alone." This widely held assumption is why, when we talk of healing the land, we invariably talk of protecting it, of preserving it. It is why we think of wilderness as the healthiest land out there—because it is the most protected. It is why virtually every environmental organization has the word "protect" in its motto or mission statement.

This assumption—that the only way we can heal the land is to protect it—isn't just the domain of activists in the environmental trenches, it is woven into the very essence of our society's awareness of what we call "the environment." It is so all-pervading and so ingrained that most of us don't even think of it as an assumption. We think of it as a matter of fact, like gravity. That's why articles that deal with land issues treat the word "protecting" as having the same meaning as "healing" or "restoring." It is why those articles never explain how protecting the land will heal it, because those two concepts are considered by so many to be identical. It is why we never hear about the ill effects of protection, because there shouldn't be any if protecting and restoring and healing are identical.

We make this assumption—that environmental problems can only be solved by reducing the impacts of humans—because we also assume ("believe" might be a better word; some of us would say "know") that all environmental problems are caused by humans. In fact that's what an environmental problem is—something that humans have done that has interfered with the natural workings of things and has thrown them out of whack, something like logging old-growth forests, overgrazing the grasslands, polluting the rivers, industrializing agriculture. We don't think of butterflies or deer or wolves as creating environmental problems. We don't even think of floods or other natural disasters as doing so, except in cases where we assume that we humans have messed things up so horribly that those perfectly natural events take on an unnatural scale.

Needless to say, successes such as those created by the members of the Lost Tribe appear to contradict this assumption. They certainly seem to provide examples of actions by humans that benefit the land, that even outperform the Leave-It-Alone approach. In a society that prides itself on being realistic, results-oriented, focused on the bottom line, one might assume that getting results of the sort I have described to you would be enough to change

This is the essence of contemporary environmentalism— this assumption that the only way we can really heal the land is to protect it from impacts created by humans: to "leave it alone."

that assumption. Instead, all they served to do for me and the members of the Lost Tribe was to illustrate the power of a prejudice.

As I continued to run up against the brick wall of the Leave-It-Alone assumption, something that was very disturbing to me as an environmentalist became very clear. I realized that no matter how impressive the results the members of the Lost Tribe were able to achieve, even if they were able to do something more impressive than get native plants to grow on a pile of rocks laced with cyanide and crusted with salt, the best they could hope for was a verdict of "Close, but no cigar." Leaving the land alone would always be assumed to have worked better. This meant that results, no matter how dramatic, weren't going to be enough to bring about the paradigm shift necessary to add the methods of the Lost Tribe to the environmental toolbox, or to even give them an unbiased trial.

The hard-to-accept conclusion is that, to our contemporary way of thinking about the environment, the health of a piece of land or a collection of ecosystems is not a matter of their condition. It is purely a matter of how that land is managed.

This, in turn, convinced me of something that I still have trouble accepting, something that is very difficult, almost impossible, to communicate to anyone who considers him- or herself to be a friend of the environment (which, by the way, includes just about everyone I know). This hard-to-accept, hard-to-communicate conclusion is that, to our contemporary way of thinking about the environment, the health of a piece of land or a collection of ecosystems is not a matter of their condition. It is purely a matter of how that land is managed. More specifically, it is purely a matter of the extent to which it is managed according to the assumption that the only way we can heal the land is to leave it alone. If a piece of land is being left alone or "protected" from human use, as in the case of a park or wilderness, to the majority of us, it is healthy by definition, no matter what its condition. If it is "used" by humans to produce something for our benefit, crops or other products, for instance, it is considered to be unhealthy—again, no matter what its condition. This is true even if the "used" land is a virtual cornucopia of birds and fishes and other diversity.

In other words, the Leave-It-Alone assumption has brought us to the absurdity that the actual condition of a piece of land is irrelevant to determining if it is healthy or not.

Just how irrelevant was made clear to me at a meeting of a group named 6-6 (for 6 of "us" and 6 of "them") in the grasslands south of Tucson, Arizona. There were actually about thirty in attendance. We had stopped at a point between the Whetstone and Mustang mountains to discuss ways ranchers could work with environmentalists to heal landscapes like the 60,000-acre ranch we were touring, when the rancher who was our host made a high-risk offer to the environmentalists present.

"Tell me what you'd like this place to look like, and I'll make that my goal and work toward it," he offered, "and that way we can be allies instead of adversaries."

After a moment of hesitation, one of the environmentalists who had represented himself as a radical—an Earth First!er—responded.

"There's only one thing you can do to make this place better," he replied. "You can leave. Because if you stay, no matter what you do to the land, no matter how good you make it look, it will be unnatural and therefore bad. And if you leave, whatever happens to this place, even if it becomes as bare as a parking lot, it will be natural and therefore good."

The respondent made that reference to the rancher making the land look good, and about it ending up "as bare as a parking lot," because he had been along on enough of these

PHOTO: DAN DAGGET

tours to have seen both. He said what he said because he wanted the rest of us to know he had taken all of that into consideration and still didn't consider it to make any difference.

As extreme as this statement seems, it shouldn't come as a surprise. After all, you and I have been reading as much in the environmental literature for decades.

In his book, *Nature as Subject: Human Obligation and Natural Community*, environmental philosopher Eric Katz calls the idea that humans can restore natural environments to a degree of health and function equal to unmanaged habitat "The Big Lie" and describes it as arrogance.

Another environmental philosopher, Peter Elliot, writes that no matter how effective a human-created restoration is, it is a failure. That even if someone restores an area to exactly what it was before humans disturbed it, it is of less value than an otherwise identical area that has not been disturbed.

You don't need to look at the area in question in order to make that judgment. What could you see that would make it false?

Nothing.

That's how these statements make the environment irrelevant. Both can be confirmed without ever looking out the window. Both are true no matter what the condition of the land. While these environmental philosophers are speaking of something they call "value"

Just how irrelevant contemporary environmentalism had made the environment was made clear to me at a meeting of a group named 6-6 (for 6 of "us" and 6 of "them") in the grasslands south of Tucson, Arizona.

instead of health, the implication is clear: They are talking about better, and to most of us, when it comes to environments, "better" or "more valuable" means healthier, more properly functioning.

Logicians would tell us that the condition of the land is irrelevant to the truth or falseness of these statements because they constitute a definition. "Rain is water falling from the sky" is a definition. It is true no matter what is happening out the window.

Because these statements are definitions, they can't be confirmed or denied by science. Scientists can only test hypotheses that are, well, testable—that can be verified or falsified by monitoring matters of fact, by collecting data and using it to confirm or deny the hypothesis. Definitions are true no matter what the data.

The Leave-It-Alone assumption thus leads us to the absurdity of an environmentalism that not only makes the condition of the land irrelevant to a determination of whether it's valuable or not, but also gives us a determination of land health that isn't testable by science.

What, I wondered, would Leave-It-Aloners say if some member of the Lost Tribe managed an area to a state of health and diversity that far outstripped a similar area that had been left alone? Would they still call this a failure? And if they did, what would that tell us about the Leave-It-Alone movement? An example wasn't hard to find.

On a working cattle ranch (the U Bar) in southwestern New Mexico, David Ogilvie

This riparian area along the Gila River is now home to the largest known population of the southwestern willow flycatcher, an endangered species, and two threatened species—the common black hawk and the spikedace.

has managed a riparian area along the Gila River to such a state of health that it:

- is home to the largest known population of one endangered species (the southwestern willow flycatcher) and two threatened species—the common black hawk and the spikedace (a fish);
- supports significant populations of several other rare species, some of which are candidates for listing;
- is inhabited by the highest density of nesting songbirds known to exist anywhere in North America; and
- has one of the highest known ratios of native to nonnative fish (99 percent to 1 percent) in the Southwest.

Ogilvie restored an area of riverside habitat that had been severely damaged by flood to a condition known, because of previous experience on the U Bar, to be especially friendly to the southwestern willow flycatcher. As a result, the endangered flycatcher population in that restored stretch of habitat increased from zero in 1997 to twenty-three pairs in 2002. At the time, that was the fifth-largest population known. Recently, a population of a species of frogs listed as threatened was discovered on the ranch, too.

The real measure of the environmental value of Ogilvie's management is best revealed, however, by comparing the flycatcher population of the U Bar's riparian habitat to two nearby preserves that combine to make up a comparable amount of similar habitat. In 2002, scientists counted 156 pairs of southwestern willow flycatchers on the U Bar. The two preserves had a combined total of zero!

When I mentioned this to a well-known environmental activist and author, he said he didn't view this as a success at all. He viewed it as equivalent to creating a garbage dump that attracted grizzly bears and calling that dump good bear habitat. (I assure you that the U Bar is no "garbage dump." To decide for yourself, take a look at the accompanying photos.)

In other words, to proponents of the Leave-It-Alone assumption, an area in which no endangered flycatchers chose to live was better habitat for that species, if that land was managed according to their prejudice, than an area that hosted the largest population anywhere.

From this it became laser-clear to me that, in order to bring about the paradigm shift necessary to add the methods of the Lost Tribe to the contemporary environmental toolbox, or to shift the way most of us define land health from a matter of how the land is managed to a matter of land condition, it was going to take more than exceptional results, no matter how striking or how hopeful.

That made me a student of this brick-wall-like assumption I had been beating my head against for years. It inspired me to study its characteristics to try to determine why this apparent absurdity—that the condition of the environment is irrelevant to determining whether it is healthy or not—was accepted so uncritically and defended so steadfastly.

One of the first realizations that came to me is that the Leave-It-Alone assumption has a good story, a simple story that is easy to understand and easy to recall. Whenever anyone confronts an environmental problem or an environmental issue, the Leave-It-Alone response comes to mind like a leg jerk after a rap on the knee:

The Leave-It-Alone assumption is woven into our very concept of nature, of what nature is and how we are related to it. It is nothing more than our culture's story of the creation of nature—the story of the Garden of Eden—adopted as policy.

Humans cause environmental problems, everybody knows that, so all you have to do to solve environmental problems is reduce the impacts of humans, or…

"Doc, it hurts when I do this."

"Don't do that."

What else do you need?

I also realized that the Leave-It-Alone assumption is woven into our very concept of nature, of what nature is and how we are related to it. It is nothing more than our culture's story of the creation of nature—the story of the Garden of Eden—adopted as policy. The Garden of Eden story is the establishment, within our culture, of the assumption that humans are separate from nature, that we are not a part of it, and that we are not animals but something different. Lots of people who consider themselves to be irreligious or even antireligious subscribe to this piece of religious dogma.

The Great Plains of North America with its huge herds of bison are offered as another proof of the effectiveness of the Leave-It-Alone approach.

Leave-It-Alone solutions are popular with our urbanite society because they produce results that make sense and appeal to urban sensibilities. For urbanites there are basically three kinds of land: 1) land that has buildings on it; 2) land that's going to have buildings on it—in other words, vacant lots; and, 3) parks. To most urbanites, rural land looks like a park, so it should be managed as such.

The Leave-It-Alone approach would turn all the world into an urban landscape of land with houses on it, land that is going to have houses on it, and parks. Where do things like food come from in this sort of landscape? From where they have always come, for urbanites—from someplace else, across the tracks, out of sight, Mexico. No problem.

Last but not least, the Leave-It-Alone assumption has proof that it works that is of a sort that appeals to contemporary sensibilities. That proof exists in the form of those large iconic, romantic, exotic landscapes such as the Amazon and the Great Bison Plains—the places we urbanites all think of when we think of unspoiled nature or what the land ought to be.

Virtually all history books and environmental writings tell us that before Columbus stumbled onto the Western Hemisphere, there were so few humans here that, with the exception of a few population centers like what we now call Mexico City, the land was a wilderness, an Eden of biodiversity and balance. At the pinnacle of this western Eden was the Amazon, one of the most diverse habitats the planet has ever known. The Amazon, the story goes, existed in this state of pristine nature because it was populated by peoples who were too few and too primitive to significantly alter its condition.

The Great Plains of North America with their huge herds of bison are offered as another proof of the effectiveness of the Leave-It-Alone approach. As the story goes, the wild and free bison were hunted by Indians who were too few to keep the Great Plains from becoming one of the most biologically productive habitats the earth has ever produced and one of the greatest successes of the Leave-It-Alone approach. Our environmental literature tells us that there are plenty of other examples of this, uncounted areas in the Americas and around the world that have remained natural and healthy because they have been unaffected or little affected by the hand of humanity. And these icons of the Leave-It-Alone approach serve as irrefutable evidence that the approach works and that it can work again.

With that in mind, I thought of the Tiptons living in their Pink Panther, and I realized that the obstacle they and the other members of the Lost Tribe will have to surmount is certainly no small one. At the same time, it became clear to me that, to get a response from environmental leaders and the general public other than "don't call us, we'll call you," their case will have to be knee-jerk simple and based on a precedent that is as woven into our way of thinking about nature as Adam and Eve being tossed out of the Garden. It will have to offer modern urbanites something that they value as much as leaving the land alone. And it will have to offer an example of its success—a proof that it works—as impressive as the biodiversity of the Amazon and the teeming fecundity of the Great Plains.

I was thinking of how difficult that challenge will be and how I might approach it as an advocate for the Lost Tribe when the fates provided an unexpected leg-up in the form of a scandal. Our society loves a scandal, especially one in which the powerful and famous are shown not to be what they claim to be, and this one fit that mold exactly. The scandal was revealed to me in an article which reported that evidence of the handiwork of gardeners had been discovered in the most hallowed halls of Eden. ■

CHAPTER TWO

EVIDENCE OF GARDENERS IN EDEN

THE AMAZON AS CULTURAL ARTIFACT ■ STRAIGHT AS A RIFLE SHOT

SELF-RENEWING SOIL ■ COUNTERFEIT ICONS (FALSE ADVERTISING)

A MAP OF EDEN ■ WILD AND MUTUAL KINGDOM

STEPPING OUT FROM BEHIND THE BLINDERS

I was having dinner with a couple of friends one night when one of them asked, "Have you seen the latest *Atlantic Monthly*? It has an article in it that you might be interested in. It's named '1491.'" I filed that heads-up in my mental get-to-it-later list and had almost forgotten about it when out of the blue I began receiving e-mails about the article from a surprisingly diverse mix of people—from ranchers, agency people, environmentalists, advocates for indigenous peoples, New Agers and so forth.

I took the hint. I read the article, and it was like discovering something I'd been looking for, and waiting for, for a long time. There it was, as plain as could be—the fracture in the brick wall that members of the Lost Tribe and I had been beating our heads against for years. In eye-opening examples, data, analysis, quotes, and citations, the article by Charles Mann struck right at the heart of the Leave-It-Alone assumption. Most exciting for me, many of those quotes concerned the Eden that served as the poster icon for the Leave-It-Alone approach—the Amazon.

"Indian societies had an enormous environmental impact on the jungle. Indeed, some anthropologists have called the Amazon forest itself a cultural artifact—that is, an artificial object," Mann wrote.

"[T]hey [Indians] were so successful at imposing their will on the landscape that in 1492 Columbus set foot in a hemisphere thoroughly dominated by humankind."

And…

"'I basically think it's [Amazonia] all human-created,' Clement told me in Brazil. He argues that Indians changed the assortment and density of species throughout the region. So does Clark Erickson, the University of Pennsylvania archaeologist, who told me in Bolivia that the lowland tropical forests of South America are among the finest works of art on the planet. The phrase 'built environment,' Erickson says, 'applies to most, if not all, Neotropical landscapes.'"

Mann also quotes Peter Stahl, an anthropologist at the State University of New York at Binghamton, who says, "[W]hat the eco-imagery would like to picture as a pristine, untouched Urwelt [primeval world] in fact has been managed by people for millennia."

Evidence that led Mann and the people he was writing about to come to these conclusions included "an archipelago of forest islands, many of them startlingly round and hundreds of acres across. Each island rose ten or thirty or sixty feet above the floodplain, allowing trees to grow that would otherwise never survive the water. The forests were linked by raised berms, as straight as a rifle shot and up to three miles long."

"It is Erickson's belief," wrote Mann, "that this entire landscape—30,000 square miles of forest mounds surrounded by raised fields and linked by causeways—was constructed by a complex, populous society more than 2,000 years ago."

Among the most striking of the several examples Mann presented were some curious areas of highly fertile soil in the Amazon that scientists believe were created by humans. This soil, according to Mann, covers "at least 10 percent of Amazonia, an area the size of France," and has the curious capability of being able to regenerate itself. By being capable of self-regeneration, this terra preta, or "dark earth" as Mann's sources named it, is able to resist the depletion of nutrients caused by the huge amounts of rainfall the tropics receive. (Tropical soils are notoriously poor because of this.). Residents of the areas where this soil persists still carry away portions of it to use "as potting soil." In spite of 2,000 years of this sort of depletion, the soil continues to regenerate itself.

In his article, Mann relates that when William I. Woods (a soil geographer at Southern Illinois University) told him that humans had created this self-renewing soil (terra preta), he said that he was so amazed that he "almost dropped the phone," and that he "ceased to be articulate for a moment and said things like 'wow' and 'gosh.'"

"Faced with an ecological problem," Mann concluded, "the Indians fixed it. They were in the process of terraforming the Amazon when Columbus showed up and ruined everything."

"It is Erickson's belief," wrote Mann, "that this entire landscape… was constructed by a complex, populous society more than 2,000 years ago."

PHOTO: COURTESY CLARK ERICKSON, UNIVERSITY OF PENNSYLVANIA

Mann and the scientists he interviewed for this article believe that other habitats in the Western Hemisphere that were likely created by humans include the bison plains of North America.

"Rather than domesticating animals for meat," Mann wrote, "Indians retooled whole ecosystems to grow bumper crops of elk, deer, and bison." They did this, Mann tells us, by reshaping entire landscapes, using fire "to keep down underbrush and create the open, grassy conditions favorable for game." Their efforts were so successful that "The first white settlers in Ohio found forests as open as English parks—they could drive carriages through the woods."

Lost Tribers were heartened by Mann's article because it meant that someone else, someone with credentials and credibility, confirmed that what they claimed to be able to do—manage ecosystems so they would be as good as, if not better than, unmanaged ones— was not only possible but that it had already been done, and with great success. The icing on the cake was that Mann claimed this had been achieved in the heart of the area used as proof by Leave-It-Aloners that the only way to heal the land is for humans to have no impact on it. Having this printed in a respected mainstream magazine made the members of the Lost Tribe a little less lost, a little less invisible.

Mann's article even seemed to refer to the Lost Tribers themselves, in a roundabout sort of way:

"If they [mainstream environmentalists] want to return as much of the landscape as possible to its 1491 state," Mann wrote, "they will have to find it within themselves to create the world's largest garden."

Or contact members of the Lost Tribe.

Mann's characterization of some of the techniques used by the original Gardeners of Eden even served as a fairly close description of what contemporary Lost Tribers do. Most

Mann's characterization of some of the techniques used by the original Gardeners of Eden even served as a fairly close description of what contemporary Lost Tribers do.

of the Lost Tribers I know are ranchers who work with "whole ecosystems" and "entire landscapes" on ranches that incorporate thousands, even hundreds of thousands of acres. And most of them manage those landscapes by working with animals that range over the land in a way similar to the way wild animals do.

For the members of the Lost Tribe, Mann's article provided an infusion of energy and optimism to a reservoir that had been running low.

For the Leave-It-Alone assumption, it had a different implication. If some of the most important of the iconic landscapes offered as evidence that "the only way to heal the land is for humans to leave it alone" were, in truth, created by humans, then the people who market that strategy are, at the very least, guilty of false advertising.

Mann was aware of the problems his analysis caused for contemporary environmentalism. "[I]f the new view is correct, and the work of humankind was pervasive, where does that leave efforts to restore nature?" he asked. As he wrote that, he seems to have been unaware of the degree to which some members of contemporary society were practicing the kind of land management he describes in his article. At one point, he says that if we could learn how the microorganisms in terra preta work, perhaps some version of Amazonian dark earth could be used to improve the vast expanses of bad soil in other parts of the world. One can only wonder what he would have said if he knew that contemporary members of the Lost Tribe have been experimenting with soil microorganisms, too, collecting especially healthy examples, growing cultures of them, and inoculating these modern versions of terra preta into soils that had been severely depleted.

"The landscape of old California… was not a 'natural' landscape. It was a landscape created by people, in many ways as 'artificial' as the farmlands of Europe."

OTHER 1491s

Although Mann's article may have been one of the most visible to present evidence that humans are responsible for the creation of some of those Leave-It-Alone Edens, it certainly hasn't been the only one.

In *The Way We Lived: California Indian Stories, Songs and Reminiscences*, Native American advocate and historian Malcolm Margolin describes how native peoples shaped the plant and animal communities of old California. Because of their stewardship and its impacts, Margolin wrote, "The landscape of old California, in other words—meadows, oak savannahs, 'park-like' areas of great boled oaks and clear understory—was not a 'natural' landscape. It was a landscape created by people, in many ways as 'artificial' as the farmlands of Europe. Thus, when Spaniards and then others first arrived in California a couple of centuries ago, they did not find (as they fondly imagined) a 'pristine wilderness.' They found what was in many ways a garden, a land very much shaped by thousands of years of human history and adapted to human needs."

And they found the Gardeners of this Eden standing among their handiwork.

In his book *Cultures of Habitat*, ethnobiologist Gary Paul Nabhan describes how he discovered the connection between humans and healthy ecosystems via an eye-opening incident that involved two maps. Both maps pictured the continental United States. Both were color-coded to present different sets of data. One map, labeled "Staying Put," depicted the relative duration of human residency in an area—how long people have typically lived there without moving. The other, labeled "The Geography of Endangerment," illustrated which counties have the most species on the federal government's threatened and endangered species list. A colleague of Nabhan's at the Arizona Sonoran Desert Museum asked Nabhan to take a look at both maps without offering any interpretation or comparison.

"Suddenly I went goggle eyed," Nabhan wrote. "The fit was not perfect, but the correlation between the two patterns was undeniable. Where human populations had stayed in the same place for the greatest duration, fewer plants and animals had become endangered species; in parts of the country where massive in-migrations and exoduses were taking place, more had become endangered."

In other words, plant and animal populations have been more stable, and more diverse, where human populations have been stable and resident. Where humans were "only visitors," which is how our society defines wilderness (the type of habitat defined by our society as the most pristine, most "natural," and most hospitable to biodiversity), plant and animal populations have been less stable and less diverse. This is the opposite of what we are told by contemporary environmentalism, with its assumption that the only way to make the land natural and healthy is to leave it alone.

OTHER LESSONS FROM THE EARLY GARDENERS

These examples point toward a paradigm shift in the way we think about the environment. They provide a reason and a rationale for redefining the way we look at the

"Where human populations had stayed in the same place for the greatest duration, fewer plants and animals had become endangered species; in parts of the country where massive in-migrations and exoduses were taking place, more had become endangered."

use of nature. They provide the basis for saying "you can't have your cake unless you eat it, too."

Today, when nature is involved, many of us think of use as being identical to abuse. We think of the relationship between the health of an environment and the extent to which it is used by humans as a negative continuum. On the end of that continuum on which "use by humans" is at its highest value, "environmental health" is at its lowest. On the other end, the end on which use by humans is low to nonexistent, we consider environmental health to be at its highest value. Wildernesses where humans "are only visitors" are considered by most of us to be the epitome of environmental health.

Viewed in terms of this continuum, the way to heal any area is to merely reduce the amount of its use by humans. Granted, it's not hard to find reasons to think this way. Use by humans has decimated our ancient forests, almost wiped out the North American bison, and is devastating the Amazon rainforest. Even ancient peoples were capable of this sort of overuse. Shortly after one group of hunters arrived in North America, 73 percent of the North American genera of terrestrial mammals weighing one hundred pounds or more became extinct.

Environmental groups wage war against efforts to "use" public lands. Environmental philosophers tell us we have no right to use other species. Some characterize the use of plants and animals as "slavery." With regard to animals, when we use them for food, more than a few characterize it as murder.

Citing examples such as this, environmental groups wage war against efforts to "use" public lands. Environmental philosophers tell us we have no right to use other species. Some characterize the use of plants and animals as "slavery." With regard to animals, when we use them for food, more than a few characterize it as murder.

In cases in which the relationship doesn't involve humans, however, use isn't considered quite so much a form of villainy. In fact, it's considered to be quite the opposite. In nature we refer to use relationships as symbioses, mutualisms, or even synergies. Bees use flowers for food, and flowers use bees for pollination and reproduction, and no one calls this "slavery." Some pollinators are so essential to the reproductive function of plant species that without the "users" the "used" would almost certainly cease to exist. Predation, most of us have come to believe, is beneficial to prey populations. Wolves remove the old and ill from herds of elk, deer, caribou, et cetera, and keep those animals from overpopulating their habitat.

Rather than being the exception, some scientists are now saying that symbioses or mutualisms in relationships among species are the rule. In his book, *Nature's Magic: Synergy in Evolution and the Fate of Mankind*, Peter Corning quotes ecologist Judith Bronstein as saying "Mutualisms…have finally come to be recognized as critical components of ecological and evolutionary process…Every organism on earth is probably involved in at least one and usually several mutualisms during its lifetime."

"Symbiosis is not a marginal or rare phenomenon," writes Lynn Margulis in her book *The Symbiotic Planet: A New Look at Evolution*. "We abide in a symbiotic world."

"In the past few years," comments Corning, "new research and theoretical work on mutualism—both within and between species—has reached the flood stage."

Nature provides plenty of examples to drive this flood. In fact, it may be more difficult to find species that aren't involved in some sort of symbiosis than to find examples of those that are. These examples provide some of the most amazing stories in nature. Some are remarkable in how completely the species rely on one another—some can no longer be identified as separate individuals. Some of these relationships are striking in how much they resemble human relationships that we think of as anything but symbiotic.

One example among many that caught my eye involves a species of marine flatworm that can be found on the beaches of Brittany on the northwest coast of France. This small worm, though transparent, appears to be bright green because each individual harbors a living colony of photosynthesizing algae. The worm and algae live in a total symbiosis. The algae feed the worm by "leaking" food they produce by photosynthesis. What interests me about this is how complete the symbiosis is. It is so complete the worm no longer has a mouth but relies entirely on the algae for food. Returning the favor, the worm produces bodily waste (uric acid), which acts as a food for the algae. No one knows how this amazing association came to be. At one time an ancestor of these worms must have consumed some algae or been "infected" by them, and the association was born. Now these species even reproduce as one.

This sort of mutualism—of animals harboring photosynthetic-capable life forms which, in turn, feed them—is a common one in nature, but there are plenty of other sorts, too.

Ants of a certain species protect "herds" of aphids from predators while the aphids excrete honeydew, a milky substance derived from plant sap, which feeds the ants.

Another variety of ants—leaf cutters—harvest vegetation in large quantities and bring it back to subterranean nests where they use it to grow crops of fungi which they then use as food. E. O. Wilson has described these ants as "true agriculturists." Corning says this symbiosis is "even more elaborate than we supposed," adding that it involves a complex division of labor that is highly orchestrated, and utilizes a further symbiosis between the ants and a bacteria that produces an antibiotic that stimulates the growth of the fungus gardens and fights a parasitic mold that attacks them.

Even the lowly cow lives by means of symbiosis. Incapable of digesting the grass it eats, the cow relies on the bacteria in its guts to do it for her. We couldn't digest the food we eat without the help of the bacteria in our own guts.

In light of the ubiquitous nature of symbiosis, it seems hard to believe that many of the relationships our species has developed with our earthly coinhabitants, and with the ecosystems of which we are a part, aren't symbiotic as well. In fact, they are.

In his efforts to learn how native peoples sustained themselves in California before Western Europeans arrived, Malcolm Margolin was told by Miwok elders that one of their food staples was the bulb of the Brodiaea plant. When Margolin heard this, he thought there must be some mistake because Brodiaea bulbs are small and the plants are literally few and far between. People would get very used to being hungry, Margolin thought, if they tried to make a living off these small, widely dispersed onionlike tubers.

When Margolin asked an elder how Brodiaea bulbs could serve as a reliable food source, he was told that when the Miwok used Brodiaea bulbs as food the plants were much more common, and that they grew in dense clumps. Because of this, harvesting enough of the plants to serve as food was easy.

To determine if this could have been the case and, if so, how, Kat Anderson, an ethnobiologist, decided to conduct a test to see if the Miwok and Brodiaea plants had

In light of the ubiquitous nature of symbiosis, it seems hard to believe that many of the relationships our species has developed with our earthly coinhabitants, and with the ecosystems of which we are a part, aren't symbiotic as well. In fact, they are.

developed a symbiotic relationship. To perform this test, she planted a plot of Brodiaea plants and, when the plants matured, she harvested them as the Miwok would have harvested them. She used a digging stick to pry the bulbs out of the ground. She brushed off the dirt and the "baby" bulbs that came out of the ground attached to the larger bulbs, and then she studied the results. What became apparent over time was that Miwok harvesting practices did seem to be beneficial to Brodiaeas. That won't be a surprise to anyone who has raised a bulb garden and knows that what you do with bulbed plants to keep them healthy, vigorous, and proliferating is dig them up, break them apart, and replant them. This is what the Miwok were doing with the Brodiaeas. Poking around with the digging stick tilled the soil and broke apart the bulb clumps. Brushing off the baby bulbs broadcast them, and walking around over the bed, as a harvester would have done, tamped them into the ground and planted them.

Absent of this mutualism (the Miwok stopped harvesting Brodiaea bulbs on any significant scale some time ago), the plants have diminished in number, extent, and clump-size to the point that they no longer are a viable food source.

The Miwok performed a similar function for clams of various species in Tomales Bay near Point Reyes, California. They harvested these clams with digging sticks and scraped off the seed clams just as they did with Brodiaea bulbs. This method worked so well that at the turn of the nineteenth century, after thousands of years of Miwok harvesting, the shellfish in Tomales Bay were so plentiful that they supported a commercial shellfish industry that, according to Rob Baker in a *News from Native California Special Report*, comprised as much as 60 percent of the West Coast's shellfish business.

This clam fishery was so important that in the mid-1930s California created regulations including a "take" limit to protect it. Baker relates that "Of the three clam species that crowded its beaches in 1935 two were extinct by 1945…, and the third was barely hanging on" just ten years later.

"Biologists had viewed these clam beds as a kind of natural and self-sustaining wilderness, upon which people were intruding," Baker writes. "Nothing could be further from the truth. These clam beds were a garden, a human creation, cultivated and kept healthy by the knowledgeable activities of those who knew the land best and who had been caring for it these many thousands of years."

In the deserts of Arizona and Baja California, Gary Nabhan describes a similar mutualism between humans and a plant called sandfood. Sandfood is a parasite that grows from its point of "infection"—a spot on a root of a desert shrub more than a meter underground—to the surface. There it blooms into a flower the size of a small fried egg. This flower then matures and disperses its seeds on the desert surface. There they are separated by several vertical feet of sand from where they must eventually come to rest in order to germinate.

How then can one of these little seeds get back down through all that sand to infect another shrub root and start its life cycle again? Enter a Tohono O'odham individual who intends to enjoy the sweet potato taste of this plant's wrist-thick stem for dinner. The eager diner digs to the place where the sand turns cool and moist and enough sandfood root is exposed to provide dinner and pops her main course free with a jerk. This jars the seedhead sufficiently that a number of seeds break loose and tumble down into the excavation. Some

"Biologists had viewed these clam beds as a kind of natural and self-sustaining wilderness, upon which people were intruding… Nothing could be farther from the truth. These clam beds were a garden, a human creation, cultivated and kept healthy by the knowledgeable activities of those who knew the land best…"

of these seeds lodge against the root of the host or another root that was bared in the process, and the cycle is completed. In addition, the pruning of the plant, which is what breaking off a piece of it entails, causes it to sprout additional branches at the pruning point and proliferate in another way.

Evidence of the existence of this relationship comes from the fact that, since the Tohono have left their Gran Desierto home, sandfood has gone from being plentiful enough to be a food staple to being a candidate for endangered species status.

For the Miwok and the Tohono, "You can't have your cake unless you eat it, too" isn't a quirky slogan. It's a way of life.

In contemporary environmental literature, however, the only way humans are described as benefiting wild species like Brodiaeas or sandfood is by protecting them, by leaving them alone or causing someone else to leave them alone. Because so many of us, even so many of our scientists, subscribe to the Leave-It-Alone assumption, mutualism between humans and other species is considered to be a pipe dream, an apology, a Madison Avenue–style cover-up for the exploiters. People who say this is possible, such as the members of the Lost Tribe, are dismissed as lackeys of industry or the political right wing, or as obvious wackos.

Consider the environmental philosopher who called the idea that humans can restore natural environments to health and function "The Big Lie" and described it as arrogance, or the other one who told us that even if humans restored a piece of land to exactly what it was before it was damaged, it was a failure.

What kind of feedback would convince them that humans could participate in a symbiotic relationship with any part of nature? They have made it very clear the answer is, "None."

Consider the environmental activist who compared the rancher's riparian area that was the home of all those southwestern willow flycatchers to a garbage dump that attracted a bunch of grizzly bears. What degree of success would have convinced him that the rancher was actually benefiting the birds? Again, the answer is, "None."

Recognizing mutualisms between humans and nature requires stepping out from behind the blinders of the Leave-It-Alone assumption. So does receiving the feedback that makes those mutualisms work. If the Miwok had harvested the Brodiaea bulbs in a way that was harmful, the Brodiaeas would have suffered and the Miwok would have gone hungry. Because they don't have a written history, we don't know if that happened or how it happened. We can conjecture one thing, however. If there had been a Miwok who said, "The only way you can heal those Brodiaea clumps and clam beds is to leave them alone," and the tribe had listened, most likely we would never have heard of the Miwok. ▪

Because so many of us, even so many of our scientists, subscribe to the Leave-It-Alone assumption, mutualism between humans and other species is considered to be a pipe dream, an apology, a Madison Avenue–style cover-up for the exploiters.

U Bar Ranch, Cliff Gila Valley, New Mexico

CHAPTER THREE

ECHOES OF EDEN – BEYOND SYMBIOSIS TO SYNERGY

THE BIRDS DON'T WANT TO LIVE OVER THERE ALL BY THEMSELVES

DON'T RUN OVER THAT FISH! ▪ NONE IS THE LONELIEST NUMBER

(IT'S A PRETTY BAD SCORE, TOO) ▪ THE SYNERGY-MINUS-ONE TEST

SPILLOVER SYNERGIES ▪ HUMANS AS A KEYSTONE OF GAIA

In his book *The Desert Smells Like Rain: A Naturalist in O'odham Country*, Gary Nabhan describes two oases in the Sonoran Desert on opposite sides of the Mexican border. One of those oases is named A'al Waipia by the Tohono O'odham Indians and lies on the U.S. side of the border. The U.S. Park Service, which has included this collection of pools and springs within the boundaries of Organ Pipe Cactus National Monument in southernmost Arizona, calls it Quitobaquito. The other oasis, which is located thirty miles south of the border in Mexico, is called Ki:towak by the Tohono people who still live and farm there.

Each oasis is formed by springs of cool, sweet water that bubbles up out of the desert and flows along small channels toward central ponds that are surprisingly large in a land this dry. Water-loving plants cluster around the ponds and the streamlets that feed them. Migrant species use the oases as a stopover. Endangered fish swim in some of the streamlets and pools. Rare and not-so-rare birds flit among the trees and rushes.

These cool ponds and the lush habitats that surround them have served for millennia as a magnet to all life that inhabits or travels through the area. Humans are no exception. Evidence suggests that both of these oases have supported human settlements since our species arrived in the area thousands of years ago. That chain of stable habitation stopped for A'al Waipia (Quitobaquito) in 1957 when the Park Service condemned the Tohono O'odham farms clustered around the spring and destroyed the houses, sheds, fences, and corrals associated with those farms.

The chain of stable habitation stopped for A'al Waipia in 1957 when the Park Service condemned the Tohono O'odham farms clustered around the spring and destroyed the houses, sheds, fences, and corrals associated with those farms.

The other oasis, Ki:towak, continues to be inhabited. When Nabhan paid the visit to Ki:towak that he describes in his book, it was the home of a Tohono community whose oldest resident was Luis Nolia, a Tohono farmer. At the time, Nolia grew summer field crops, kept an orchard and a few animals, and harvested medicinal plants that grow wild in the moist habitat surrounding the springs.

In order to do this more effectively, Nabhan tells us, Nolia performed a number of tasks to help the habitat provide what he needed. He plowed and irrigated some of the land nourished by the springs. This, in turn, expanded the habitat that supported at least six species of wild greens, including plants that the Tohono regard as having medicinal value. He removed debris from the springs and from the streamlets just as he removed it from his own irrigation ditches. He planted willow cuttings on the banks of the pond from which he later harvested willow whips to make "leafy crosses" that hung on the walls of every household in Ki:towak. He planted elderberry, salt cedar, date palms, and the California palms that shaded his house. He cultivated the wolfberry, mesquite, and palo verde that formed a hedge on his field edge. He planted cuttings from ancient fig and pomegranate trees into more open areas, where they produced rewards for both Tohono and wildlife. The planted willows stabilized the banks of the pond. The hedges provided cover, nesting areas, and insects for birds and cottontails. All of these actions of stewardship have benefited both human and nonhuman inhabitants of the oasis.

Providing a sharp contrast, says Nabhan, A'al Waipia, across the border in the U.S., which has been managed as a preserve since 1957, serves as "a cool, shady sanctuary where we can sit and watch birds, and ponder over a little pond filled with endangered desert pupfish." Nabhan reports, however, that there is trouble in this Park Service paradise. "[A]n odd thing is happening at their 'natural' bird sanctuary," he writes. "They are losing the heterogeneity of the habitat, and with it, the birds. The old trees are dying. Few new ones are being regenerated. There are only three cottonwoods left and four willows. These riparian trees are essential for the breeding habitat of certain birds. Summer annual seedplants are conspicuously absent from the pond's surroundings. Without the soil disturbance associated with plowing and flood irrigation, these natural foods for birds and rodents no longer germinate."

According to Nabhan, in three years of back-to-back visits to A'al Waipia and Ki:towak he and a crew of ornithologists counted less than half as many birds at the preserve as they did at the area that was farmed.

For an explanation of this apparent anomaly, Nabhan asked someone whom he thought would know more about it than a university-trained scientist. He asked a Tohono farmer why there were more birds at the farm than there were at the preserve, a place that had been set aside "just for the birds." The farmer gave an answer that was plain and straightforward: "When the people live and work in a place, and plant their seeds and water their trees, the birds go live with them. They like those places; there's plenty to eat and that's when we are friends to them," he said.

ANOTHER FRIEND TO THE BIRDS

Farther north, along the Gila River in southwestern New Mexico, a rancher named David Ogilvie has had a similar experience. When he first noticed flashes of red, yellow, and blue in the trees in some of the fields and pastures he manages along the Gila, his feelings were mixed. Seeing those birds made him feel good because he knew they hadn't been there when he came, and he was sure they were there now because of something he had done. But the birds were a cause for worry, too.

The ranch Ogilvie manages is the U Bar. It is owned by the copper mining giant Phelps Dodge, which has a large mine in the area. The year before Ogilvie noticed the increase in birds, he had started water flowing again through a system of dirt irrigation ditches constructed by previous owners of several small ranches that Phelps Dodge had purchased and consolidated to create the U Bar. One of the responsibilities Ogilvie had been given when he took the job to manage the U Bar was to maintain the water rights associated with it. When mining operations experienced a drop in water needs, Ogilvie was instructed to put the water to some productive use in order not to lose the right to it. In the West, the law that applies to water is "use it or lose it." Ogilvie decided to rewater the ditches to irrigate some of the croplands and pasture of those old ranches.

The year before Ogilvie noticed the increase in birds, he had started water flowing again through a system of dirt irrigation ditches constructed by previous owners of several small ranches that Phelps Dodge had purchased and consolidated to create the U Bar.

As water flowed back into the ditches, they leaked, as all dirt ditches do, and trees growing along their banks began to revive. The trees had been able to reach maturity partially because they were protected from wildfire by the cattle who ate the grasses that might carry a fire to them. Some were protected from being uprooted by floods by the earthen levees maintained by the ranch. Nourished once again by water from the ditches, the trees sent out new shoots, leaf canopies thickened, seedlings began to appear, and the birds came.

Along with the birds came the worry. Ogilvie was aware that more than six hundred miles of river and streamside in the Gila drainage (including the riverside land on the U Bar ranch that he managed) had been identified as possible habitat for the endangered southwestern willow flycatcher. Since some of the people calling for protection of the flycatcher were also calling for the removal of cattle from all habitat that could potentially

The largest population yet discovered of the endangered southwestern willow flycatchers–64 pairs–were counted on the U Bar in 1995.

support the bird, Ogilvie was concerned that, if some of the birds flitting through those recently revitalized trees were flycatchers, it could mean that he would have to remove the cattle from those pastures. Reflecting on the irony that a blessing as obvious as an increase in songbirds could be a source for worry, he decided it would be good to find out just where the U Bar stood.

With that in mind, he hired a biologist to do a bird survey. What the biologist found was a cause for both pride and concern. The biologist reported that he had not only found southwestern willow flycatchers among the U Bar's recently

PHOTO: COURTESY U.S. FISH AND WILDLIFE SERVICE

revitalized trees, he had found the largest population yet discovered—64 pairs of endangered flycatchers were counted on the U Bar in 1995. In that same year 38 pairs had been counted along the Kern River in California, the next most populous site. Over the next two years, the numbers at the U Bar increased dramatically (for an endangered species). In 1996 the number was in the 80s. In 1997 it broke 100.

Those high numbers caught the attention of a number of people, including Dr. Scott Stoleson, wildlife biologist for the Rocky Mountain Experimental Station in Albuquerque. Stoleson's curiosity was engaged by the apparent anomaly that, on the U Bar, the largest population of flycatchers was cohabiting with what was supposed to be their nemesis—cattle. Stoleson undertook a detailed study of the U Bar's riparian habitat and its otherwise rare flycatchers. Those studies indicated that what is happening on the U Bar is neither an accident nor an anomaly. On the contrary, it seems that Ogilvie's ranching practices have tended to promote and sustain the kind of habitat these endangered birds prefer.

When the southwestern willow flycatcher was listed as endangered, it was believed that the birds preferred dense willow thickets as habitat. Dr. Stoleson has found that, rather than dense, undisturbed stands of willows, these rare birds prefer patches of mature cottonwoods and box elders with a relatively open understory. That's exactly the kind of habitat found on the U Bar.

The conventional wisdom has it that man-made irrigation ditches are also a put-off for flycatchers. Stoleson's observations reveal that proximity to water is the second most significant factor in the birds' choice of a nest site, and the vegetation-rimmed ditches of the U Bar suit that requirement to a T.

When it comes to their supposed nemesis, cattle, the U Bar flycatchers do more than tolerate them—they seem to prefer them. Stoleson's data shows that areas on the U Bar that are grazed by cattle support more flycatchers than those that aren't grazed. And the flycatchers that nest near cattle are more prolific than those that don't. In fact, the U Bar's flycatchers are the most naturally prolific population known. From 64 pairs in 1994, the U-Bar population grew to a high of 200 in 1999. At the time, Stoleson says, the ranch was home to 40 percent of the entire known population of this subspecies.

In 2000, southern New Mexico experienced a severe drought, receiving only 34 percent of its average annual moisture. That year only 130 pairs were counted at the U Bar, but the birds that survived were hard workers. "Nest success was the highest ever that year," said Stoleson. "Sixty-seven percent of nests fledged at least one young. That's the highest rate ever recorded on a site where there is no predator control." Since then, the drought has continued, but the population has recovered to 137 pairs in 2001 and 156 in 2002.

As surprising as the U Bar's flycatcher community is, it's just part of the ranch's rare species success story. As Scott Stoleson and a few other scientists began taking a closer look at the U Bar riparian area, they found that it serves as home to the highest density of songbird territories yet measured in North America—an average of 1,300 territories per one hundred acres. The next most dense site supports 1,100. Other TES (threatened, endangered, or significant) species doing well on the U Bar include the common black hawk, Abert's towhee, Bell's vireo, Gila woodpecker, Gila chub, desert sucker, and Sonoran sucker. Evidence exists that on the U Bar stretch of the Gila, 99 percent of the fish are native species and only 1 percent nonnative. The average for other streams in the Southwest is closer to the reverse of that. Studies indicate that within the U Bar's riparian habitat, you will find the largest known population of one threatened fish, the spikedace, and among the largest populations of another, the loach minnow, both of which are listed by the Nature Conservancy as among the five hundred most endangered species in the U.S.

What these rare animals seem to be telling us in the most significant way they can—by making their homes and proliferating on the U Bar stretch of the Gila—is that this riparian area on a cattle ranch is managed in the way best suited to ensure their survival and promote their recovery.

A couple of other striking facts illustrate just how strong is the endorsement these birds are giving the U Bar. Two preserves, one upstream and one downstream of the U Bar, provide a habitat for the birds that is free of cattle. In 2001 and 2002, when the U Bar accounted for 137 and 156 pairs respectively, the protected areas hosted only 7 pairs in 2001 and none in 2002.

As surprising as the U Bar's flycatcher community is, it's just part of the ranch's rare species success story…it serves as home to the highest density of songbird territories yet measured in North America—an average of 1,300 territories per one hundred acres.

To prove that the tendency of flycatchers to choose the U Bar over the preserves wasn't a fluke, Ogilvie decided to create some habitat that embodied the birds' preferences. At the time the ranch was working to repair damage caused by two years of flooding (in 1993 and in 1995). As he stood on the edge of the flood, watching rich bottomland soil being undercut and washed away, Ogilvie thought this might be an opportunity to show that ranch operations could be designed to benefit flycatchers as well as the ranch. When the levees were reconstructed and contoured, Ogilvie instructed the workers to leave backwaters and

When we learned that the birds were doing so well along those irrigation ditches, in a habitat that was basically artificial, I decided I wanted to do something special to show that a ranch really could create flycatcher habitat.

TOP PHOTO: COURTESY U BAR RANCH

multiple channels to provide the kind of slow-moving waters flycatchers like. He also had the bulldozer operator plant large cuttings of willow and cottonwood along the river's edge to provide habitat for the birds when the waters went down and the place returned to normal.

"When we learned that the birds were doing so well along those irrigation ditches, in a habitat that was basically artificial, I decided I wanted to do something special to show that a ranch really could create flycatcher habitat, so I did this," Ogilvie said.

Seven years later, 23 pairs of flycatchers were counted on "the Bennett," named for the old ranch that occupied the area before it was incorporated into the U Bar. "That's the fifth largest population known," Ogilvie told me as we searched for flycatchers among the twenty- to thirty-foot-tall trees the cuttings had become.

In spite of those impressive results on the U Bar, the Final Recovery Plan for the southwestern willow flycatcher models its approach on the protected areas. In fact, a second project that would have enlarged the U Bar's successful habitat restoration even further did not receive the required U.S. Fish and Wildlife Service approval until the grants that would have funded it had lapsed.

When I visited the U Bar for the second time with photographer Tom Bean, we visited the U Bar's habitat and one of the preserves I mentioned above, an area downstream of the U Bar named the Bird Area.

On the U Bar, Tom and I were guided by Ogilvie and Kathy Broadwell, a U.S. Fish and Wildlife Service biologist charged with monitoring the flycatchers. Also along on that trip was Ty Bays of Phelps Dodge. We visited a number of areas during that trip, including the place where Ogilvie did his habitat restoration. As we walked, Broadwell told of an instance in which she was looking into a low brushy area in close quarters, trying to see if a bird might have made a noise she heard. As she peered into the brush, a mountain lion stepped out. She also told us about being shadowed by a black bear that made a couple of bluff-charges at her. She was trying to stay out of the way of both of these animals and still do her job of monitoring the birds.

Tom and I were guided by Ogilvie and Kathy Broadwell, a U.S. Fish and Wildlife Service biologist charged with monitoring the flycatchers. Also along on that trip was Ty Bays of Phelps Dodge.

During our visit, the riparian area watered by the flow of the Gila was vividly green and lush. The rest of the ranch, however, showed the apparent strain of a prolonged drought. It rained a few times while we were there, and Dave's "unofficial rain gauge," a puddle on the lane to his house, filled to overflowing. "When the puddle's full, that means we got a half-inch," Dave said.

We saw a few flycatchers, though not as many as on my other trip, and we saw a number of nests and got some wonderful photos, but the most revealing part of this visit was a trip to the Bird Area, one of the preserves that borders the U Bar. Tom and I had scheduled a tour of the area with Ralph Pope, who administered the preserve for the U.S. Forest

Service, but a day or two before that appointment we found ourselves with nothing to do, so we decided to check it on our own.

As Tom and I neared the preserve, its "flycatcher score" relative to the U Bar kept running through my mind—U Bar 156, Bird Area 0 (in 2002). I wondered what the place looked like. "It must not look very good," I thought, since so few flycatchers live there. I also wondered how the upcoming encounter with Pope would go. I had published the comparative scores of the Bird Area and the U Bar in a number of places, and I wondered how he had taken that. I was pretty sure he had read what I had to say, and I know people don't like to have their work presented in a bad light. I know I don't.

When Tom and I arrived at the Bird Area, I was surprised at how beautiful it looked. The trees that grew along the river were big and lush and healthy. Grasses and sedges grew in profusion on gravel bars and on the stream banks. In places where the river slowed and pooled, it was cooled by the shade of overhanging limbs. Logs and stumps that had washed into the pools and eddies formed hideouts for fish. Smaller trees of varying sizes and species formed thickets in the area between the riverbank and an abandoned farm field back from the river.

The area looked so good I wondered why more of the rare flycatchers didn't live here.

A couple days later Tom and I had our meeting with Ralph Pope. Right off the bat, he took care of the questions I mentioned earlier. First, he dispelled my concern about whether or not this would be an adversarial encounter. Pope was entirely at ease, obviously

The trees that grew along the river were big and lush and healthy. Grasses and sedges grew in profusion on gravel bars and on the stream banks. In places where the river slowed and pooled, it was cooled by the shade of overhanging limbs.

confident of his abilities and comfortable with
the work he had done. Second, he answered
my question about why there weren't more
flycatchers here.

"We've got lots of moving water here,"
he said. "Don't have much of that slow water
with trees nearby that Scott found out they
like so much up on Dave's place."

As he described some actions that were
being taken to try to remedy that situation, it
became apparent that Ralph Pope based his
actions on feedback rather than assumptions.
He spoke of his high regard for Dave Ogilvie
and told us that, here on the preserve, the

*"We've got lots of moving
water here," he said.
"Don't have much of
that slow water with
trees nearby that Scott
found out they like on
Dave's place."*

Forest Service was applying some of what Ogilvie and Stoleson had learned about flycatcher
habitat on the ranch, and that it was having good results.

"We've used a bulldozer to dig some potholes back from the riverbank behind the
trees. We dug 'em deep enough that they'd fill with subsurface flow from the river and maybe
have the same effect as Dave's backwaters."

The three of us fought our way through thick stands of cottonwood saplings that
crowded the potholes. Pope blamed a long-standing drought for the fact that they had dried
up before our visit, but said the effort appeared to be having some success anyway.

"We got a few birds singing here this year," Pope said as we pushed our way through
the saplings. "None of them nested, but that's still an improvement. Maybe next year."

Back at the vehicles, Pope talked about some of his other experiences in this
biodiversity hot spot. He lamented the contentiousness of the endangered species wars and
told some great stories about the absurdities such contentiousness can cause. One of his
stories involved one of the most bizarre situations I have ever run across. It was a situation I
had become involved in, too, and Ralph Pope's anecdote shed some personal light on one of
its most outrageous aspects.

A TALE OF TWO RIVERS

This story started for me with a conversation I had with some people from the range
management staff of the Prescott National Forest (PNF) and some ranchers in the Verde
River Valley of central Arizona. We were discussing a project for which I felt I could get grant
support via EcoResults!, a not-for-profit I had formed in my efforts to crack the Leave-It-Alone
monolith. What we all wanted to do with this money was to revitalize some deteriorated
rangeland within the Verde watershed. No problem there. There was plenty of that.

As we discussed possible sites for the project, one of the PNF staffers mentioned
that we would have to cross the Verde River to get to some of the areas that we all agreed
needed the treatment most. That, he said, would be unwise because it would require getting

regulatory approval, which would take a minimum of five years and could even delay the project permanently. If a project requires regulatory approval, he told me, its chances of being approved are so far out in the future that the Forest Service places it so far down on its priority list that we would probably give up before it ever happened. Better for EcoResults! to find support for a project that had already been approved, they advised, even though that project may not exactly fit our goals. If it had already been approved, it wouldn't have to run the impassable gauntlet of regulatory approval.

There's a problem with this… The Verde River was listed as home to a threatened fish—the spikedace. That meant the U.S. Fish and Wildlife Service (USFWS) would have to be consulted before the tree clipper could be transported across the river.

To make sure I adequately appreciated the difficulty involved here, someone said, "Tell him about the AgriAxe."

The group told the story in chorus. Each contributed what to him or her was the most outrageous component. The story, as I understand it, goes as follows: The ranch had permission to do a forest-thinning project on Forest Service land south of the river (the river I had been advised not to try to cross), in an area that was seriously degraded. Although this area had once been a grassland, it had deteriorated for a variety of reasons, until it had become a monoculture of widely dispersed juniper trees with little to no understory. Because of this lack of understory the area was losing soil rapidly. Eventually, there was a good chance it wouldn't even support the trees.

All the regulatory requirements had been satisfied for the tree-thinning that was intended to return this area to the grassland it once was. Public input had been collected, questions answered, and archaeological clearance completed. A plan of action had been formulated. Arrangements had been made to rent the machinery needed to do the work. Everything was ready to go when someone realized that the main machine, a tree clipper named an AgriAxe, would have to be hauled across the Verde River on the only road left open to the project location. All other roads into the area had been closed by a Clinton Administration program to reduce the number of roads in remote areas.

There's a problem with this, the storytelling chorus explained. The Verde River was listed as home to a threatened fish—the spikedace. That meant the U.S. Fish and Wildlife Service (USFWS) would have to be consulted before the machine could be transported across the river. Some group, I was assured, would surely object to driving the truck across the river because it might run over one of the threatened fish. That, I was told, would constitute a "taking" (killing) of a TES species under the Endangered Species Act. Without a permit agreed upon in advance through consultation with the USFWS, this would be a violation of federal law. Engaging in such a consultation could take a very long time and would most likely result in a lawsuit, so the project, though approved, was essentially dead. It had become such a can of worms that the Forest Service would no longer devote any time to it. "We've got a lot of things to do that are a higher priority than this," one of the Forest Service staffers told me.

"But the crossing is on my private property," Dave Gipe countered. "I drive across the river every day, and you guys [pointing to the Forest Service personnel sitting among us], you drove across the river today when we went up to look at where these guys want to do their project. You didn't consult with the Fish and Wildlife Service to do that."

"That was just us doing our job," one of the Forest Service staffers replied. He then explained that the AgriAxe project would involve using federal money and therefore would constitute a "federal action." This, he explained, requires USFWS consultation where it involves endangered species. Somehow this made it different from driving across the river as we had done a few minutes earlier.

At this point George Yard, who owns a ranch farther downstream, piped up: "But there hasn't been one of those fish seen on the river for five years."

This introduced another aspect of this controversy that took it from the absurd to the ridiculous. It seems that several years prior to the meeting I am describing, the decision had been made by the Forest Service, on the advice of the USFWS, to remove all cattle from public lands along the upper stretches of the Verde (which was the great majority of land along that part of the river) in order to keep cattle from having a negative impact on the river and therefore on the fish. For nearly a century previous to that, cattle had grazed along the Verde, eating streamside vegetation—cottonwood and willow seedlings, grasses, and rushes—so the riverbanks remained sparsely vegetated and in some areas denuded. Without grazing, the idea went, the riparian area would be less disturbed, which would make the whole area more lush and more "natural," and enable the fish to avoid extinction and maybe even increase. Among the threats that would be removed by banning cattle from along the river, some pointed out, was the threat of a spikedace being stepped on by a cow or accidentally swallowed by one while it was taking a drink.

Removal of cattle was completed in 1997, with rancher George Yard volunteering to keep cows off his private land along the river, too. The year 1997 was important to this story for another reason. It was the year of the last confirmed sighting of a spikedace on the upper Verde.

Every year since 1997, scientists have continued to use nets and electric "fish shockers" to monitor fish populations (as they did before the removal), and every year since 1997 they have come up spikedaceless. Not only that, they are finding that populations of other native fishes, which had been doing well on the Verde, have begun dropping as well.

What connects all this to the U Bar is that the Gila River, at least where it flows through the U Bar, is very similar to the Verde. It's of similar size and flows through a similar desert habitat. One big difference, however, is that where the Verde seems to have lost its spikedace population, the Gila still harbors a healthy population of the fish. In fact, it is home to the largest concentration of spikedace known to exist anywhere. One of the pieces of that spikedace heaven is actually on a small tributary of the Gila, Mangas Creek, at a ford—a place where cars regularly cross the creek. When someone told me this, before I had seen the place, I envisioned a crossing where the creek is deep, and you have to drive slowly in order to avoid the willows and clumps of grass that grow out into the stream. How else could it be home to a large population of a fish that is so slow, sluggish, stupid, and unaware that it could be stepped on by something as plodding, noisy, and avoidable as a cow slogging through water?

However, when I saw that piece of spikedace heaven, my picture of a lazy, natural ford was shattered. The Mangas Creek crossing is anything but quiet and pristine; it is a shallow strip of flowing water with no vegetation on either side. A gravel road goes straight across

Every year since 1997, scientists have continued to use nets and electric "fish shockers" to monitor fish populations (as they did before the removal), and every year since 1997 they have come up spikedaceless.

This piece of spikedance heaven is anything but quiet and pristine. It is a shallow strip of flowing water with no vegetation on either side.

the stream and continues, just as straight, into the countryside. The first time I saw it, even though the concrete slab that forms the roadbed had been washed out (as is frequently the case), you could still take the crossing at almost twenty miles an hour, and it looked like some people did. Any fish that picks this place as its number-one habitat is pretty good at not getting run over by either a cow or a truck hauling an AgriAxe, I thought. In fact, when I saw the place, I joked that any fish that chooses to live here must do it because it likes to surf the wakes cars make as they go blasting through. I could imagine little spikedaces bodysurfing a car wake far onto the streamside gravel beds and then wriggling their way back down into the creek to catch the next wave.

As we leaned on our trucks in the parking lot of the Bird Area, Ralph Pope revealed that he was the one who discovered this spikedace hangout. He told how one day, while driving the road leading to the Bird Area, he saw a man at the ford seining for minnows to use as fishing bait in a nearby lake. Ralph stopped for a chat and realized, as the man lifted his seine from the stream, that a lot of fish in the seine were spikedace. Back home, he made a phone call to John Rinne, one of the scientists studying native fishes in the Southwest, and told him he might want to take a sample at the ford.

Rinne came to Mangas Creek and dipped his seine into the pool at the crossing. When he pulled it up out of the water, he was shocked at how many fish it contained. "It was so nice to dip into that little place and come up with oodles of fish," he said. Rinne said he counted from 400 to 500 spikedace that day and the farther he got from the crossing the fewer fish he found.

Rinne offered a reason the spikedace had done so well in such an unlikely place. Spikedace prefer habitats with lots of "fines"—extremely fine particles of sand and mud,

Rinne said. So do other small native southwestern minnows. These fish use fines for nesting, and they forage through it when it is stirred up, he explained. Dave Ogilvie says he has seen so many of these small fish swarming behind bulldozers in the river doing flood control work that they remind him of descriptions he has read of California coastal grunion runs.

This leads us to what scientists say may be the reason spikedace have become so rare on the Verde but not on the Gila. The Gila drains a steep, rocky watershed that frequently sends large floods downstream. The Verde drains a much flatter area that floods less frequently and less violently. Scientists speculate that the frequent floods on the Gila keep the riverbed disturbed to the extent that adequate fines are available to keep the spikedace happy and plentiful. Floods do not perform that function on the Verde, or at least they don't perform it as well.

In spite of this, a number of people say that what the spikedace on the Verde need in order to rebound is a large flood. If you apply the calculus of synergy, however, another possibility arises.

SYNERGY MINUS ONE

One way to tell if a synergy exists, according to Nathan Corning, is by noticing that, when a major part of some whole or system is removed or breaks down, the whole breaks down. In fact, one way to test to see if a set of relationships is synergistic is to remove one of the parts and see what happens. If the system changes dramatically, most likely it was synergistic. Corning calls this test "synergy minus one."

When cattle were removed from riverside habitats along the Verde, the whole broke down—spikedace disappeared, and populations of other native fish began to drop. That could be an accident, but it also could be an example of synergy minus one. There is evidence that supports the latter.

When cattle had provided continuous disturbance along the Verde, grazing and even overgrazing its banks, much of the riverbed had looked a lot like that ford on Mangas Creek—wide, shallow and gravelly, most likely with a good supply of fines. Now, with the cattle gone, the trees, freed from the cattle's grazing, had grown and spread, crowding the riverbanks and causing the Verde to run narrower, deeper, and cooler. This not only reduced the amount of disturbed areas available for producing fines for spikedace, it also increased the amount of habitat ideal for smallmouth bass and flathead catfish. These nonnative species are deadly predators of small fish. Many of the natives in the Verde are small. All are small when they are young.

Since one way to destroy a synergy is to remove one of its vital elements, it would seem to follow that a way to restore that synergy would be to re-include that part. That would also serve as a way to test if that part was really the one that made the system work in the first place.

Although local ranchers along the Verde and even a few scientists have suggested trying this course—returning grazing and its impacts to the river to see if this would bring back the spikedace—the wildlife powers-that-be continue to wait for their flood. So, in 2004, the

Since one way to destroy a synergy is to remove one of its vital elements, it would seem to follow that a way to restore that synergy would be to re-include that part. That would also serve as a way to test if that part was really the one that made the system work in the first place.

situation stands at seven years and counting, and everyone has begun to wonder if there are any fish to bring back.

SPILLOVER SYNERGIES

The examples of the Tohono farmers of Ki:towak, Dave Ogilvie's positive experience with the flycatcher, and the spikedace that continue to exist on the Gila not only add to the case that humans can have mutually beneficial relationships with nature, they take that case a significant step further. These examples reveal that humans can create mutualisms with nature that go beyond the one-on-one of Miwok and Brodiaeas or Tohono and sandfood. They indicate that humans can create mutualisms that benefit a diversity of life forms across entire ecosystems.

Coral reefs are immense structures that are basically the product of a mutualism or symbiosis involving three tiny marine creatures—coral polyps, a type of alga, and something called a dinoflagellate. The skeletons of uncountable generations of this symbiosis actually form entire islands in the South Pacific and even the bedrock of some parts of the ocean floor in that area. Whole areas of this warm sea have been described as "living beings" because of the immensity of the reefs that inhabit them and the profusion and diversity of life those reefs host and support. The symbiosis that has created and sustains this magnificent wellspring of life is a simple one. The coral polyps secrete urea and other nutrients that nourish the algae and dinoflagellates, both of which return the favor by supplying the polyps with food and certain minerals. The polyps, thus nurtured, secrete the calcium structures that serve as a home for themselves and their symbionts and uncountable other creatures. Without this mutualism, none of the three main players in this collaboration would exist, nor would the reefs, nor would many of the islands of the South Pacific.

That, in itself, is an amazing achievement, but what takes this association beyond symbiosis to synergy is the fact that living among, around, and on the structures created by the skeletons of this partnership is one of the richest diversities of life the planet has assembled anywhere. Reef fish, sea urchins, eels, sea snakes, lobsters, marine worms, sharks, palm trees, tropic birds, dolphins, humans, and other critters too numerous to name live among the reefs and islands formed by this humble symbiosis. Synergy has been described as a relationship in which one plus one equals more than two. Here is an instance in which one plus one plus one adds up to a sum that defies calculation or even description.

The U Bar and Ki:towak obviously haven't reached reef status, but they are in the same ball game. In both places, the benefits of a central mutualism spill over to benefit other species. For some of us, the fact that humans are involved in these examples makes comparing them to a coral reef an absurdity, sort of like equating garbage dumps and reefs, but the ultimate expression of mutualism—the Gaia Theory—tells us that on planet Earth all life forms work together to create and sustain the conditions without which life could not exist. Plants transform carbon dioxide into oxygen, which animals and plants use to turn their food into energy. Both then respire carbon dioxide back into the air as a waste product of their digestion. The cycling of water from oceans into clouds and rain cools the planet

Coral reefs are immense structures that are basically the product of a mutualism or symbiosis involving three tiny marine creatures…without this mutualism, none of the three main players in this collaboration would exist, nor would the reefs, nor would many of the islands of the South Pacific.

and stabilizes its temperature, creating conditions more amenable to life than the sizzling days and frigid nights of our nearest planetary neighbors. Life makes the conditions for life available to life. Life sustains life. That is the means by which life exists on Earth. The true absurdity would be to believe that humans don't participate in this planetary mutualism, or at least that we didn't participate before we started acting like aliens.

The stories of the ranchers of the U Bar and the farmers of Ki:towak help lift the blinders of the Leave-It-Alone assumption to show us that indeed we can participate in this work, and that we can do it, not as a bit player but as an important player, even a keystone. These stories also make us better able to recognize instances in which we still are a part of the functioning mutualism we call nature, or can become a part of it again. In some instances they can even instruct us on how we can become part of it for the first time.

This is no small favor. If we're not aware of being part of a mutualistic relationship, there's little to stop us from ignoring it, crippling it, or even destroying it—consider the story of the spikedace and the Verde. Also, if we're unaware that we are part of a synergy, there's little chance that we will be an effective part of it, or that we will know how to restore it if it begins to unravel. Last, but not least, if we don't know (or don't believe) that humans can have relationships with nature that are mutually beneficial, we won't spend much time working to create that kind of relationship, nor will we have much success if we do.

Having made this realization, the next challenge becomes applying it. Once we recognize the synergies of which we are a part, we can fix the ones that are busted and create new ones where it is in our interest and in nature's interest for us to do so. ▪

The stories of the ranchers of the U Bar and the farmers of Ki:towak help lift the blinders of the Leave-It-Alone assumption to show us that indeed we can participate in this work, and that we can do it, not as a bit player but as an important player, even a keystone.

El Coronado Ranch, Arizona

CHAPTER FOUR

DROUGHTBUSTERS

TRINCHERAS AND TRINCHERITAS ▪ EFFECTIVE RAINFALL
POOPING AND STOMPING ▪ STOPPING A FLASH FLOOD WITH
GRASS BLADES ▪ HOW MANY TIMES ARE WE GOING
TO HAVE TO LEARN THIS LESSON?

There have always been people who would like to make it rain more in the West, only now there are more of them. The reason is because the West is in one of the most serious droughts it has experienced since we began recording such things. In parts of the region, the drought is in its seventh year and shows no signs of letting up. In some places, the total is said to be nine years and counting. The year 1996 was described as the driest year ever recorded in Arizona.

Among the impacts of this monumental drought are some of the worst wildfire seasons in history, reservoirs dropping to historic lows, drought-weakened trees succumbing to insect infestations they would normally be able to resist, wildlife numbers dropping, crops failing, and farms and ranches going bankrupt. Here in Arizona, whole mountainsides of trees are dying, Lake Powell is at its lowest level since it was filling for the first time, and the state experienced the largest wildfire in its history just one year ago—half a million acres of forest burned in one monstrous conflagration.

Humans have been trying to make more rain fall from the sky for probably as long as we've been able to think in such terms. We've danced, prayed, sung, made sacrifices, hired rainmakers, sent smoke up into the clouds, dropped chemical crystals into them, and still the amount of rain that falls has remained, over the long run, a matter of the discretion of God or nature or good fortune.

Although humans haven't had much success at making more rain fall, we have had considerable success at making what has fallen more available to the plants, animals, and ecosystem processes we depend on.

In the essays "Song of the Gavilan" and "Guaycayama," in *A Sand County Almanac*, pioneer ecologist Aldo Leopold describes a trip he took in the early 1900s to the watershed of the Rio Gavilan in the state of Chihuahua in northern Mexico. Leopold wrote that what impressed him most about this watershed was how it had been altered by past residents to more effectively utilize the scarce precipitation that fell there. Those previous residents had done this by constructing an absolutely amazing number of trincheras (terraces) or small, loosely piled rock dams in all the watercourses within the watershed.

"Ascend any draw debouching on any canyon," wrote Leopold, "and you find yourself climbing little rock terraces or check dams, the crest of one level with the base of the next."

By the time Leopold visited the area, the builders of those trincheras had been gone for some time, and the beneficiaries of their handiwork were wildlife rather than people. Leopold reported seeing 180 deer in nine days. A year later, on a subsequent visit, he saw 250 deer in sixteen days. Remember, this isn't Pennsylvania, it's the Chihuahuan Desert.

Sixty years later, Gary Nabhan retraced Leopold's footsteps to the Rio Gavilan and described the visit in his book *Cultures of Habitat*. Nabhan found the trincheras still there, still doing their job, and still benefiting wildlife rather than people. He also found the area still as wild and unspoiled as Leopold had described it.

Nabhan notes that Leopold was so impressed with what he saw on the Rio Gavilan that he said it was here he "first clearly realized that the land is an organism, that in all my life I had seen only sick land, whereas here [on the Gavilan] was a biota still in perfect aboriginal health." Nabhan reported that after his experiences with those trincheras, Leopold included land that contained "the appropriate presence of cultural features set in place by inhabitants" (that's how Nabhan put it) in his concept of "unspoiled wilderness."

TOPMINNOWS, MONKEYFLOWERS, AND MUD TURTLES

Not too far west of the Rio Gavilan, in Mexico on the Rancho de los Ojos Caliente, and to the north in the U.S. on the western slopes of the Chiricahua Mountains on El Coronado Ranch, Joe and Valer Austin, ranchers and conservationists, are singing a similar song. The Austins are responsible for building tens of thousands of trincheras that range in complexity from a stick or rock or two, placed strategically where erosion is just starting, to huge gabions made of rock-filled wire cages spanning watercourses nearly a hundred yards wide.

Carefully but loosely hand-placed, at least in the cases of the nonwired rock piles, these trincheras are designed to slow water rather than stop it. For that reason they have less of a tendency to wash out than would a dam. As the water slows behind the rocks, it drops whatever sediment it happens to be carrying—soil particles, pine needles, leaves, animal dung, and so forth—to form organic-rich sponges that absorb water and make it available to water-loving plants that colonize these sediment deposits. These sponges slowly release the water they have captured, lengthening the amount of time the stream flows and the amount of time the water is available to life along its course. Valer says some streams that were dry for nine months of the year now flow for as long as they once were dry.

The Austins' rock piles have thus turned what were barren gullies and flash flood expressways into a series of terrace gardens

Trincheras are designed to slow water rather than stop it. For that reason they have less of a tendency to wash out than would a dam.

PHOTO: COURTESY OF EL DORADO RANCH

Rock piles have thus turned what were barren gullies and flash flood expressways into a series of terrace gardens inhabited by wispy, nodding deer grass, delicate maidenhair, colorful monkeyflowers, and more.

inhabited by wispy, nodding deer grass, delicate maidenhair, colorful monkeyflowers, and more. The rock piles create small pools upstream, where water slows as it winds its way through them, and downstream where it digs small basins as it pours over the piles. These pools, some of which retain water except during the deepest of droughts, provide homes to minnows, frogs, toads, and turtles, as well as a variety of insects, microscopic life, and water-loving plants. The value of these mini-oases is hard to estimate in a region where water is known to be an infrequent and tempestuous visitor, and where riparian areas play an important role in the lives of 80 percent of the wildlife species. Several of the species that inhabit these veins of green are threatened or endangered or at least rare. Among the rare species that have benefited from the Austins' trincheras are Gila topminnows and Sonoran mud turtles.

The Austins are no strangers to this work of benefiting endangered species. They funded efforts to restore the thick-billed parrot to its former range in the United States, and they built a research facility on El Coronado that houses research, monitoring, and quarantine equipment as well as personnel. When I was there the facility was being used to quarantine rare Gould's turkeys prior to their release into the U.S. where they had been extirpated earlier in the century.

The most ambitious of the Austins' restoration projects is in an area south of the Mexican border in the once-edenic San Bernardino Valley. Before overuse and mismanagement degraded and desiccated this valley, it was a marshy grassland or *cienega* with artesian springs bubbling out of the ground. Here, in this marsh-become-desert, the Austins have built their largest water-slowers, the ones made of huge wire cages filled with hundreds of tons of rocks.

The head of one environmental foundation has called this project "the most important biodiversity restoration in North America." When I visited the area, bulldozers were reshaping the land to remove the grossest changes brought about by more than a century of mismanagement. At that time some of the Austins' gabions had been in place for a year or so. Some, including the largest of all in Silver Creek, had just been completed. Behind those that had been in place for a couple of years, frogs "urped" in midjump before they plopped into the water. Turtles, up for a breath of air, went "down periscope" and hurried out of sight.

Gabions have a history of failing.

PHOTO: DAN DAGGET

In the middle of this area, a pond watered by an artesian well was being sculpted to serve as a *refugio* for native fish. Some of those fish were already present. They darted into deeper water as we walked by.

The Austins are aware that their effort is a gamble. Gabions have a history of failing. I've taken plenty of pictures of big ones left high and dry by flows that hurried around, over, or under them, or just ripped them to shreds. One of the Austins' gabions had already suffered a fate of that sort. Its middle had slumped into a tunnel the water had dug under it. "The soil in this area has a tendency to form 'pipes,' you know, like tunnels," Joe Austin said as we looked at the wire-bound rock pile, sagging in the middle like a stick someone had stepped on.

Later, as we drove from one site to another, Valer added, "Joe exaggerates what he does. He does way more than what others would do; way more than what others say he should do. He doesn't do one or two gabions, he does lots of them. Not all of them last, but that doesn't mean they don't work."

The Austins' smaller efforts fit my sensibilities more. There's something very grounding about walking along in the middle of nowhere and looking down and seeing a stick or a rock placed in a little erosion rill to stop it from deepening. That feeling of groundedness grows as I look downslope and see scores of these little structures crisscrossing the gully as it winds out of sight. Actually, "structures" seems to be the wrong word here. These little water-slowers look more like art than industry. And because they are high in the watershed, and because there are thousands of them (the Austins stopped counting at 20,000), they can have a greater impact than something much larger farther downslope, the way a small object close to the light can throw a larger shadow than something much larger farther from it.

Encountering one of these works of eco-art in an out-of-the-way place inspires a feeling of connectedness with other people, to people from other times and other places who used sticks and stones instead of complex technologies to solve environmental problems and achieve environmental goals. Trinchera systems like the one Leopold observed along the Rio Gavilan are common around the world. They grace watersheds in China, Nepal, Peru, Yemen, Vietnam, Malta, Australia, and the islands of the South Pacific, as well as here in the southwestern U.S. Virtually everywhere humans have farmed, they have created terraces.

The urge to slow water seems almost to be a part of our essence. Maybe the urge has been around long enough to have become incorporated into our genes. As a kid I loved to pile rocks and pieces of cutbank sod to make little dams in creeks on farmlands near my home in Ohio. After making those dams we (usually my cousin and I) would splash around, as much as we could, in the small pools they made. The real pleasure, however, came from looking at the water we had backed up and feeling a sense of accomplishment and connection. My wife, Trish, remembers having the same experience playing in streams out back of her suburban home in Cincinnati, Ohio.

There are those who would disparage this and say what I am describing here are inappropriate feelings of arrogance after having imposed my power on nature, but I didn't feel arrogant; I felt connected, included, at home. After all, nature builds trincheras, too.

These little water-slowers look more like art than industry. And because they are high in the watershed, and because there are thousands of them, they can have a greater impact than something much larger farther downslope.

She builds her own water-slowers, and she generally enlists the help of some agent to do so. Sometimes those agents are humans.

I tried my hand at making trincheras on a project in the watershed of the Verde River, the river of the disappeared spikedace. The project involved, among other people, Al Medina, the scientist with the Rocky Mountain Research Station in Flagstaff, Arizona, who commented on the Tiptons' heap-leach project. Medina honed his skill at trinchera building while working with a number of different communities, from the White Mountain Apaches in southern Arizona to the people of Salvemos al Rio Laja (Save the Rio Laja), in Guanajuato, a state in central Mexico.

Medina has gained a reputation as an outside-the-box thinker. The Verde River attracts that kind of person—the conundrum of the spikedace is partially responsible for that. But the Verde also has thwarted its share of in-the-box solutions to other problems, including the use of gabions to stop gully-cutting. Rather than being stopped by those rock boxes, the gullies of the Verde have left them high and dry, but no one has made as many of them as Joe Austin would.

Medina's approach to healing gullies involves a lot of observation—a lot of walking their twisting courses trying to see what inhibits as well as what abets their formation. On those walks, Medina says he has noticed that all gullies reveal deposits or "lenses" of rocks and gravel at regular to varying intervals along their course. Streams do this, too, of course, alternating riffles with pools. Figuring that the ecosystem must have had some reason to put rocks where it put them, Medina places his loose piles of rock where he sees these natural deposits. "I let the ecosystem tell me where to put my little rock piles," he says. Medina makes his riffle trincheras low, wide, and loose, from bank to bank, and shaped like a broad, shallow "V" with a low spot in the middle. He does this because, just as in the case of the Austins' trincheras, the piles are meant to slow the water rather than stop it, to absorb its energy rather than to confront it.

Over time, the space upstream of these piles fills with sediment and debris and is colonized and stabilized by plants. Once the new soil is stabilized, another layer of rock may be added and then another, until the gully essentially fills itself (with a little help). This approach requires monitoring the system and coming back and building new rock piles, perhaps several times. "We give the system what it needs, when it needs it, and no more," Medina observes. "We do this because we have learned that to solve problems in nature, we have to apply processes, not remedies."

This may be a hard sell in our quick-fix society, but it has yielded excellent results on the White Mountain Apache Reservation and in the Rio Laja watershed in Mexico, where the idea of working with the land is not as far removed as it is from second-, third-, or fourth-generation urbanites in the United States.

Medina and I decided to join forces on the project in the Verde because we each had ideas on water-slowing that appealed to the other. We picked our target via consultation with the collaborative team of ranchers, scientists, and federal and state land managers who were involved in that conversation about the AgriAxe and the spikedace I described earlier. In fact, this was the project that resulted from that conversation.

This approach requires coming back and building new rock piles, perhaps several times. "We do this because we have learned that to solve problems in nature, we have to apply processes, not remedies."

We decided to try our methods on a small meadow that was being desertified by a gully formed along the course of an old dirt jeep track. Having sliced a gash into the meadow for most of its length, the gully was lowering the meadow's water table, much as a drainage ditch de-waters a swamp. As a result of that de-watering, the meadow's grasses were disappearing, being replaced by weeds or bare dirt, and erosion was accelerating. At some point in the not-too-distant future, the gully would claim the entire area, and it would be hard to tell there had ever been a meadow here.

Medina's part of the project was designing and supervising the building of the trincheras. My part included stabilizing the newly deposited soil behind the trincheras and reversing the desertification process on what was left of the meadow. To do this, I intended to use the technique used by the Tiptons to restore that heap-leach pad in Nevada. In fact, we used the Tiptons as consultants on the project. Their job was to show us how to use cattle to get grass to grow on land that was desertifying, just as they had used cows to get grass to grow on mine waste.

On a more fundamental level, my intent with this project was to further test the idea that humans can create "spillover synergies," and that we can use the mutualistic relationship that includes us, and grazing animals, and the grasses and soils that support those animals (and us) to create results that benefit a long list of other species. In other words, I was doing this project to test the hypothesis that humans and grazing animals can play the same role as a coral reef.

Large animals break up plant litter and tramp it onto the ground. Rain floats this litter along until it wedges between a couple of grass blades, and—Voila! You have a mini-trinchera. A trincherita!

One of the functions I believed animals could play in this project was to create other water-slowers in addition to the ones Medina would build. From my experience with the Tiptons and others who use the same techniques, I knew that large animals moving in herds break up plant litter (old plant stems, dried blades of grass, et cetera) and tramp it into the ground as they move across it. When enough rain falls to create even a minimal flow across the land, it picks up this litter and floats it along until it wedges between a couple of grass blades or rocks or the ridges of a hoofprint or whatever, and—Voila! You have a mini-trinchera. A trincherita!

PHOTO: DAN DAGGET

Trincheritas perform the same function as those rock piles on the Rio Gavilan and at El Coronado Ranch, albeit on a smaller scale. They slow the runoff, causing more water to be absorbed by the soil. And they capture other little pieces of litter and debris to form small litter jams (as in logjams), where the latter retains moisture and decomposes to form soil. Individually, the effects of these trincheritas are tiny, but multiplied over millions of instances, their effects can be significant.

From the Tiptons' experience on that heap-leach pad and on various other projects they had completed successfully, we knew animals could also create the conditions for more plants to grow on parts of the meadow that had desertified. At the time of this project, members of the Lost Tribe had been employing this technique long enough, and successfully enough, that it had been given a colorful name. Courtney White of the Quivira Coalition, an environmental group in Santa Fe, New Mexico, calls this technique a Poop-and-Stomp. The cows eat and stomp what they don't eat into the soil, along with seeds that were either there naturally or were broadcast, and as they graze they poop and stomp that into the soil, too, providing fertilizer and inoculating the soil with microfauna. All this leads to more grass.

Range scientists and other people who think about such things maintain that the stems and roots of plants provide one of the most important routes for water to enter the soil. Gregg Simonds, a private consultant known as one of the more progressive and successful rangeland managers in the West, estimates that as much as 80 percent of the water that enters the soil enters via a plant stem.

The plan, then, was for Medina to build his trincheras to stop the gully from cutting deeper and to cause it to begin to fill itself with sediment deposited behind the rock piles. The

We hauled rocks to the site and built the trincheras under Medina's direction. My EcoResults! partner, Norm Lowe, and I spread the seed, and the cowboys of Dave and JoAnne Gipe's Rio Verde Ranch spread hay and brought the cows.

PHOTOS: DAN DAGGET

Poop-and-Stomp would initially form trincheritas to further slow runoff and impede erosion on the meadow. As a delayed result, it would get more grass to grow to further impede runoff and provide routes for the water slowed by the trincheritas to enter the soil. As a result of all this, the gully would heal and the meadow would be returned to function. Simple as that.

To make an already long story a little shorter, we got a grant from the U.S. Environmental Protection Agency via the Arizona Department of Environmental Quality, hauled rocks to the site, and built the trincheras under Medina's direction. My EcoResults! partner, Norm Lowe, and I spread the seed, and the cowboys of Dave and JoAnne Gipe's Rio Verde Ranch spread hay and brought the cows. The animals did their job eating and scuffing and trampling the hay and seeds into the rocky desert dirt as they fertilized it. And then we removed the cows and waited.

And as we waited, a couple of things occurred to me that hadn't occurred before. For the first time, I realized that it's a lot more risky to perform restoration projects than to write about them. In other words, I realized that I had a real stake in the success of this project, and I realized it on a gut level as well as a cerebral one. As a writer, if a restoration fails, you write about why it failed, or you write about one that didn't fail. Either way, you come out a winner. As a restorer, if a project fails, you fail, and you've put yourself in a credibility hole that you then have to dig your way out of.

As I think back on it now, that restoration was done in 2002, in the deepest part of a nine-year drought. That no doubt added significantly to my anxiety level.

Because that year was a dry one, as so many have been recently, I was so worried (and curious) that I drove the hundred-plus-mile round-trip to the project site more often than perhaps I should have to see how things were progressing. On those trips, I passed another site relevant to the story I'm telling here—something called the Drake Exclosure. More often than not, I stopped because, more often than not, it made me more confident.

You see, the Drake Exclosure represented the competition—the Leave-It-Alone approach.

SYNERGY-MINUS-ONE ALL OVER AGAIN

In 1946 a forty-acre piece of rangeland about 100 miles north of Phoenix was fenced by the U.S. Department of Agriculture to protect it from all impact by humans, especially all utilitarian impact. The area was named the Drake Exclosure after the small community of Drake that once housed a couple thousand people who built a railroad through the area. The forty acres were fenced because the area had become so devastated in the early twentieth century by human overuse and abuse that the U.S. Forest Service decided to protect a portion of it from livestock and other human-caused disturbances so various means of healing the land could be tested. This area had been brought to its sorry state, the story continues, by more than a half-century of year-round livestock grazing, woodcutting, accidental and intentional fires, crop raising, and other activities. In other words, the area that became the Drake Exclosure had been subjected to the same sorts of abuse as much of the rest of the West. It typified rangeland conditions in the 1940s throughout millions of acres of pinyon-juniper woodlands and grasslands in the West.

As a writer, if a restoration fails, you write about why it failed, or you write about one that didn't fail. Either way, you come out a winner. As a restorer, if a project fails, you fail, and you've put yourself in a credibility hole that you then have to dig your way out of.

After the land was fenced, more than half a century ago, a number of restoration techniques were tried and the results recorded and studied. In parts of the exclosure, where the only plants that had been able to survive (juniper trees) had become a stagnant monoculture, they were bulldozed. This was done because it was surmised that the reason the land had fallen into such a state of suspended inanimation was that nothing could compete successfully with the junipers.

Next, areas where the trees had been removed, and some areas where they were left as well, were seeded with a variety of plants. These plants included both natives and nonnatives. The nonnatives were selected for their touted ability to recolonize even the most devastated land.

Last, but not least, a considerable portion of the exclosure was left untouched in order to see how well leaving the land alone would heal it.

I visited this area almost every time I drove by, to compare what was happening there to what was happening on our project. I even helped organize a field trip there. The outing included visits to both the Drake and the meadow. One of the speakers on that field trip was Al Medina.

Medina started his presentation on a part of the exclosure that had experienced no disturbance by humans since 1946.

About thirty people showed up for the field trip, including people from a variety of government agencies, both state and federal, a couple of range-management consultants, scientists, a few environmentalists, and some ranchers, including Don and Ruben Verner of the Bar Heart Ranch, which is part of the Almida Land and Cattle Company, which also owns the adjoining Rio Verde Ranch. The Rio Verde, you'll remember, was the location of that exchange about the AgriAxe and the spikedace I reported earlier. It was also the site of the meadow restoration I was so worried about.

Medina started his presentation on a part of the exclosure that had experienced no disturbance by humans since 1946. One of the first things you would notice if you visited this part of the exclosure was its barrenness. Roughly 90 percent of it was nothing more than bare dirt dotted with a mosaic of small stones. This serves as a huge surprise to many of the people I have brought to the Drake or to whom I have described this place. Almost all of them expect exactly the opposite when they hear it has been protected from cattle grazing for more than half a century.

As we looked down at the mosaic of pebbles, Medina asked us, "How many times are we going to have to learn this lesson before we finally get it?" As Medina asked this question, he swept his arms in an arc to indicate the part of the exclosure in which we were standing. Most of us were startled by the abruptness of his question. Not many talks on rangeland health start with something so "in your face." But it did get our attention.

"…if this is what we want, we know how to get it. We know that if you fence five acres or five hundred or five million, much of it will end up looking like this."

The only plants included in that arm-sweep, except for a few withered weeds, were juniper trees, some of which were as far as forty feet apart. Separating these smallish trees were large expanses of bare dirt on which the effects of sheet erosion were plainly visible. The surface that was left consisted mainly of small rocks imbedded in a crust compacted by wind and raindrops and baked by the sun into a surface ecologists call desert pavement. The nature-made pavement of the Drake closely resembles a human-made one contractors call exposed aggregate. In other words, the left-alone area of the Drake, except for the intermittent trees, looks very much like a parking lot.

Having called our attention to this, Medina continued.

"We've been doing what we've done here—putting fences around places like this so they aren't disturbed by human activity for a hundred years, and we've been watching what happens to them, and when what we see here keeps happening, we don't say, 'All right, I get it. This doesn't work.' We say, 'We need another study.'"

Medina, whose passion is apparent when he talks about things that matter to him, spoke in staccato as he leaned low and swept his hand from just above the bare ground to a series of finger punches aimed at the horizon and, presumably, into the future. "Is this what we want the West to look like?" he challenged. "Because if this is what we want, we know how to get it. We know that if you fence five acres or five hundred or five million, much of it will end up looking like this."

From the Leave-It-Alone portion of the exclosure, we moved to areas where more active remedies had been tried. Here native and exotic grasses had been seeded both where the trees had been bulldozed and in some places where they had been left alone. There were more plants and more diversity in these areas, but studies show that 90 percent of the plant species that were either here in the first place or were planted as part of some study have disappeared.

Medina asked, "If this land was being managed by a rancher and 90 percent of the plant species disappeared, what would happen to him?"

Some of us mumbled the obvious answer—that any such rancher would be in big trouble. I got his implied answer, too: Because leaving the land alone is considered only to do good, no one would be blamed for making these species die by putting a fence around them.

There are thousands of exclosures like the Drake around the West, maybe hundreds of thousands if you count all the little bent-wire cages scattered around the region to protect a couple square feet of rangeland so we can see what the land would look like if it weren't impacted by humans in various ways but mostly via livestock. Some of them, as Al Medina pointed out, have been exclosed for more than a century. In fact, Medina was the chief scientist for six years on the Santa Rita Experimental Range, a series of study areas and exclosures near Tucson that was set aside in 1903.

Not all of these exclosures are in a condition as bad as the Drake. But the point is, a lot of them are, some more, some less. The ones in the driest areas seem most vulnerable. "All of them may not show the same degree of deterioration as the Drake," Medina offered, "but they all exhibit the same processes of deterioration."

In fact, says Medina, many of these same processes are epidemic on public and private lands on areas that aren't being intentionally rested but are slowly being abandoned to become defacto Drakes. That's one thing that makes the Drake so important, because so much land across the West—millions of acres—is undergoing the same changes by means of the very same processes.

Many of these same processes are epidemic on public and private lands on areas that aren't being intentionally rested but are slowly being abandoned to become defacto Drakes.

That doesn't mean you can't find land that's being left alone that appears to be in good condition. The processes of deterioration Medina refers to can be slowed and even countered by a number of means. In moist areas—back east for instance—the simple process of rot can do it. But ecologists are virtually unanimous today in believing that ecosystems need some sort of disturbance in order to function—grasslands especially so. When the westward-expanding United States removed bison and fire from the Great Plains, one of the most extensive, most productive grasslands on earth was quickly invaded by trees. In other words, an ecosystem that had been functional for thousands of years crashed when deprived of the disturbance that had maintained it. If what you end up with as a result of that crash is a forest, maybe it's worth the loss of a grassland. But if what you end up with is the kind of barrens that are characteristic of the Drake and epidemic around the West, that's another matter.

The Drake is valuable because it provides a window into the future that can give us some idea of what the effects may be of dedicating huge amounts of land to the Leave-It-Alone solution, which is exactly what we are in the process of doing. One Leave-It-Alone group, the Wildlands Project, has advocated that as much as 50 percent of the North American continent be set aside in reserves: "set apart from human activities." Some members of this project, according to their web site, "have called for as much as 89% of our nation's land mass to be set aside in these reserves." And the Wildlands Project is considered relatively mainstream. Other Leave-It-Alone groups don't advocate setting aside that much land, not necessarily because they consider that it would do harm, but because they're

That doesn't mean you can't find land that's being left alone that appears to be in good condition. The processes of deterioration Medina refers to can be slowed and even countered by a number of means.

concerned that asking for that much would get them cast as radical. To be fair, a growing number of environmental groups are taking a broader view of this. They are pursuing solutions that are more collaborative and, therefore, more results-oriented. Still, however, the majority of environmental groups measure their success, and make their pitches for members and money, based on the amount of land and species they "protect."

What this means to me is, we are in the process of committing an immense amount of land in the American West to a form of land management—leaving the land alone—that is exempt from our environmental laws, is unstudied, has been proven to fail, and has credentials that we've recently discovered are phony. To boot, we're doing this without monitoring this approach's results, without holding it accountable, and we're committing to it forever. How do I come to that conclusion?

During that field trip at the Drake, after Al Medina had pointed out the extensive amounts of bare ground inside the Drake and how it was eroding and losing biodiversity, I made my way over to a couple of staffers of the Prescott National Forest and asked them whether they took into consideration the negative impacts of leaving the land alone when they made a decision about land use. And, if they did, I asked if they included measures to mitigate this damage in their management plans. I asked that question because the National Environmental Policy Act (NEPA) requires that any proposed action on public land must be studied to assess its impact on the environment, and, where that impact is significant, it must either be mitigated or the action can be denied.

Their answer was, "No." They didn't take the negative impacts of leaving the land alone into consideration, nor did they make provisions to mitigate its impacts. The reason, they explained, was because, according to Forest Service policy, "Rest is not considered to have negative impacts, because it is assumed to be the absence of use and therefore the absence of activities that have negative impacts."

In other words, when it comes to leaving the land alone, the feedback loops of contemporary land-management agencies are closed. There might be monitoring going on—there are monitoring transects all over the Drake and the rest of the West—but no one's reading the meter. Even when the meter is flashing in the danger zone, the interpretation is: "Oh, that can't be. Leaving the land alone can't have bad impacts. If something's wrong, it must be because of something else." The negative impacts on the Drake, the examples of sand food, Brodiaea bulbs, Tomales Bay clams, southwestern willow flycatchers, Verde River spikedace, and God knows how many other species, prove that leaving the land alone can have a significant impact—a significant *negative* impact. There is another way we can know that is the case—by contrasting the results of leaving the land alone with the competition.

Our field trip eventually took us outside the exclosure. There the scene was strikingly different. Most obvious was the fact that much less of the land was bare. Here, the distance between live perennial plants could be measured in inches rather than yards, in spite of evidence that the land had been used, and recently at that. Cattle dung and cow tracks indicated the land was being grazed at least intermittently. Stumps surrounded by scattered limbs indicated that people had been cutting trees for firewood here. Vehicle tracks leading to and from those sites showed where the soil had been disturbed and its crust broken. In spite

We are in the process of committing an immense amount of land in the American West to a form of land management— leaving the land alone—that is exempt from our environmental laws, is unstudied, has been proven to fail, and has credentials that we've recently discovered are phony

Our field trip eventually took us outside the exclosure. There the scene was strikingly different. Most obvious was the fact that much less of the land was bare. Here, the distance between live perennial plants could be measured in inches rather than yards. Left: inside the Drake looking out; below: outside looking in.

PHOTOS: DAN DAGGET

of this obvious evidence of what some people would call abuse, the land was more diverse, more productive, and more vital. There were even more rabbit tracks, gopher holes, and signs of all kinds of small animals outside the exclosure. On the inside, there were areas in which there were no tracks of any kind. Zero. Outside, the rabbit trails were traveled so well they could be described as rabbit highways. Some of them wandered a few yards inside the Drake, but they all wandered back out.

That got me to wondering if there was a corollary to the synergy-minus-one principle that could be stated: "If you add something to what was once a synergy and that doesn't fix it, what you added wasn't what was missing." That seemed to be what had happened at the Drake. We can be pretty sure this area was once grassland because of the uniform age of the trees, because of the depth of the soil and because historical accounts tell us many areas of the arid Southwest, including the Drake, once produced so much native wild grass that, in a good year, they could be harvested for hay. Now you can barely find enough grass in most of those areas to pick a stalk to chew on while you contemplate what happened here. Adding protection, or more properly, removing human impacts, hasn't restored those grasslands. The land has remained as wounded and impaired as it had been at its worst. Actually, it appears to have deteriorated more. Protection is not what was missing.

THERE'S RAINFALL AND THEN THERE'S RAINFALL

I've had a number of people tell me that the only reason there can be more grass or more plants growing in one area than another, all other things—soil, elevation, temperature, and other physical factors—being the same, is that it must rain more in one area than the other.

The two sides of the Drake Exclosure fence have the same soil, the same elevation, the same aspect, and the same temperature. In fact, they're the same in just about every way except one side has a lot more growing on it than the other. So, it must rain more on one side than the other, right?

Right.

In a very important way, it does rain more on one side of that fence, although if you put a rain gauge on both sides, they would always register the same amount.

Most of us believe that rain is rain, that one area that receives fifteen inches of rain has, for the most part, as much moisture available to its life forms as another area that receives the same amount of precipitation. Some of us are aware that there are other factors here. We're aware that how those rains come is relevant, too—that an area in which the rain comes in a few torrents, followed by long periods of hot windy days, is drier than an area in which the rains are spread over lots of days separated by temperate weather.

But there are other factors that can make a difference in rainfall. Precipitation falling from the sky can be intercepted by the canopies of trees and other plants and by the litter beneath them, causing it to evaporate without ever having reached the ground. Water that does fall on the ground can encounter a surface that either welcomes or rejects it.

According to a study by Texas A&M University, trees and the litter under them intercept 19 percent of the rain that falls. (That's why we take refuge under a tree when it

Most of us believe that rain is rain, that one area that receives fifteen inches of rain has, for the most part, as much moisture available to its life forms as another area that receives the same amount of precipitation.

rains.) On the average, only 80 percent of the water that falls on a tree finally makes it into the soil under it.

Bare dirt, without an umbrella of tree limbs and leaves over it, and with no "overcoat" of leaf litter protecting it, would thus seem to be much better off. All the rain reaches the ground here. However, the Texas A&M study tells us that bare dirt sheds 75 percent of the water that falls on it. Assuming that the Drake bare dirt and Texas bare dirt aren't all that different, that would mean only 25 percent of the rain that falls on the 90 percent of the Drake that is bare ground soaks into the soil. Since the exclosure receives an average of 12 inches of moisture a year, that means 90 percent of the left-alone part of the Drake receives only 3 inches of effective moisture a year. An ecosystem in a 3-inch annual moisture area is much, much different from one in an area that receives 12 inches. Some of the driest areas of the Great Basin Desert, the Sonoran Desert, and the Mojave receive about 3 inches of moisture a year. The average annual rainfall in the Sahara Desert is 8 inches!

Taken as a whole, the 9 percent of the Drake Exclosure that is mostly sheltered by trees receives an average of 9.72 inches of moisture a year. Mix that in with the 91 percent of the Drake that is bare dirt and receives only 3 inches of effective moisture and it means the Drake Exclosure receives only an average of 3.67 inches of rain per year even though 12 inches fall from the sky. That's dry! But that's not the only reason those lands are dry.

The lack of plants on the barren parts of the Drake had a drying effect in another way. Plants remove carbon from the air by transforming it into organic material (tissue, food, and waste). Because as much as 90 percent of a grass plant is underground, much of that organic material in a grassland ends up in the soil. There, it serves another important purpose—it absorbs and stores moisture. Any gardener knows that soil with a significant organic content is better at storing water than soil with less organic material. The barren areas of the Drake include little to no organic material and therefore are extremely ineffective at storing water. That deepens the rest-induced drought of these areas even more. No wonder they're so bare.

This is another effect that exists on those extensive acres of land affected by the same processes as the Drake because we are leaving them alone. One recent discovery that may affirm the extent of this phenomenon is a report that the loss of the land's ability to absorb and store water has accounted for as much as 30 percent of the rise of the oceans in the last century (from "Anthropogenic Disturbance of the Terrestrial Water Cycle" by Charles J. Vorosmarty and Dork Sahagian, in the September 2000/Vol. 50 No. 9 of *Bioscience*").

MEANWHILE, BACK AT THE RESTORATION

Back on the meadow restoration, the rain finally did come, and in typical Southwest fashion, some of it came in torrents. After waiting what I thought was a sufficient time for the plants to respond to the monsoon moisture, I drove down to take a look. Along the way, I stopped at the Drake. All that had grown on the left-alone parts of the exclosure were a few wispy weeds all of the same species.

As I neared the project site, I encountered evidence of just how big the rains had been. At one desert wash, my route was partially blocked by a juniper tree that had been uprooted

Because as much as 90 percent of a grass plant is underground, this organic "sponge" serves the important purpose of enhancing the ability of the soil to absorb and store moisture.

*Those piles had done
their job wonderfully.
The area upstream of
each one harbored a
deposit of sediment
sporting a thriving
variety of plants from
weeds to native grasses.*

by floodwaters and left high and dry in the middle of the road. I was impressed. Juniper trees are high desert trees. They seldom live near water. For a flood to rip one of them out by the roots, the water had to be very high.

When I came to the little meadow, it was obvious the water had been high here, too, but the evidence was of a different sort. Even in places where the impact of the cattle had been exceedingly high, the grass had grown so thick that, when the floodwaters hit these areas, the millions of blades of grass had slowed the flow and spread it. Thus slowed, the flood reacted in two ways. It dumped the debris it was carrying, spreading ropy moraines of juniper berries, pine needles, sticks, cow pies, and jackrabbit turds across the surface. And its waters soaked into the ground rather than hurrying on toward the river and wreaking havoc along the way.

Those are the functions meadows play in ecosystems—spreading, slowing, and absorbing water. In this case, the ability of this particular meadow to perform its natural function was aided by Al Medina's little rock piles. Those piles had done their job wonderfully. The area upstream of each one harbored a deposit of sediment sporting a thriving variety of plants from weeds to native grasses. Because the water had run so high, some rocks had been dislodged from a few of the dams, forming nature-made obstacles downstream. Some of the seeds we had spread on the meadows had washed off, too, but the presence of their species in the spurt of growth upstream of the dams indicated they, too, had been captured and sprouted.

In one season, this human-made restoration project had empowered the gully to fill itself at least partially with water-transported soil and litter and to stabilize that re-created meadowland with flood-resistant grasses.

As I walked farther downstream, off the project area and past that uprooted juniper, evidence suggested the water had been even higher. Here another drainage had joined the flow, and the combined streams had moved a lot of material—rock and gravel and that juniper. But where the flood had reached a large meadow just downstream of the confluence, thick, lush, and well-rooted native grasses had spread the flow, absorbed its energy, and stopped the flood dead in its tracks. Debris was plentiful, piled where the grass had stopped it. At the edge of the meadow was evidence of how effectively the collection of stems presented by all those grasses had directed the waters of the flood into the soil. Four huge ruts showed that someone had driven a vehicle a little too far off the road and sunk into what must have appeared like grassland but in reality was a swamp. The vehicle apparently had become horribly stuck and had to be dug out.

"That was Dave," Don Verner said. "We sent him up there to get the stock trailer, and he stuck 'er good. We had to use the tractor to get him out." ■

Even in places where the impact of the cattle had been exceedingly high, the grass had grown so thick that, when the floodwaters hit these areas, the millions of blades of grass slowed the flow, spread it, and stopped it.

U Bar Ranch, New Mexico

— CHAPTER FIVE —

LUB-DUB

THAT'S CPR NOT CRP ▪ DON'T YOU SMELL THAT SMELL?
THE HONEY BEAR TEST ▪ SEQUESTERING CARBON
RESTORING ONE OF THE WONDERS OF THE WORLD

My goal is to capture every raindrop where it falls," says Gene Goven, who operates a ranch in the prairie pothole country near Turtle Lake in North Dakota. Goven has undertaken this challenge on the northern Great Plains, the bison prairies, one of the icons of the Leave-It-Alone approach, an area where herds of these half-ton-plus creatures once stretched as far as the eye could see and took days to pass by.

As on that restoration project in the Verde Valley, Goven uses cattle to enhance the water-capturing capability of his piece of the Great Plains. The fact that he uses cows instead of bison affects how his effort is perceived but little else, according to Goven. Though he uses cows, Goven manages them to graze the land in a way similar to how bison might have done it. He keeps his cattle moving, keeps them from "parking" and overgrazing, and lets the land dictate the length of their stay and the time of their return, as it would do in the case of bison.

Goven's method of making his land more able to absorb and hold water has succeeded sufficiently that he has attracted considerable attention from his neighbors, government land management consultants, and scientists as well. Among the latter is Dr. Jim Richardson, a scientist at North Dakota State University.

THAT'S CPR, NOT CRP

Richardson has studied Goven's land since 1990. He has compared the rate at which water infiltrates Goven's land to land that has been grazed in a more "conventional" manner—frequently that means continuously, until winter requires the cattle to be brought in and fed hay. He has also compared it to land that hasn't been grazed at all. According to Richardson's studies, Goven has been able to increase the ability of his land to absorb water more than six times. Goven says that the water infiltration rates have changed on his ranch from early 1980, when they were 0.8 inch to 1 inch per hour, to more than 6.3 inches per hour based on U.S. Agricultural Research Service and Natural Resource Conservation Service (NRCS) monitoring.

I visited the Goven Ranch in August 2003 with Dr. Richardson, Gene Goven, Jeff Printz of the NRCS, and my photographer friend, Tom Bean. The year had been a dry one, with some good rains in March but little to none afterwards. The fact that the weather had been hot may have been a boon to our purpose because it enabled the land to show us where its water cycle was most functional. Where the land had been able to absorb and hold moisture, the grass growing on it was green. Where it had been less able to do so, the grass had cured to various degrees of yellow.

Dr. Richardson had offered to take us onto the land and give us a demonstration of its infiltration abilities. When he and Jeff Printz arrived, we drove to a point on the ranch about halfway between the top of a low hill and a glacial pothole. Richardson pulled out his sharpshooter (a long, narrow-bladed, short-handled shovel), pushed it into the soil with a firm shove of his boot, and dug about an eight- to ten-inch-deep hole. "See how easy that shovel cut into that dirt," he said. "That shows us we've got dirt here instead of concrete. The organic content of this soil, the carbon, makes it easier to dig."

Then he showed us the rich black color of the soil. "That's the carbon," he said, as he crumbled the soil with his hands. He also pointed out the profusion of roots present all the

I visited the Goven Ranch in August 2003 with Dr. Richardson, Gene Goven, Jeff Printz of the NRCS, and my photographer friend, Tom Bean. Gene's daughter Kayla and her friend Sarah Eslinger rode along to perform cowboy duties.

way to the bottom of the hole and noted the way the plug of dirt he was crumbling cracked vertically.

"These vertical striations enable water to infiltrate the land better because it can follow the striations right down into the soil. You don't see those kinds of striations on land that hasn't been grazed the way Gene's grazing it." Then he offered each of us a sniff of a piece of black dirt. It smelled like dirt to me, but Richardson and Goven pronounced its odor something more than that—sweet-smelling and healthy.

"When it's anaerobic [when it doesn't have access to the atmosphere and oxygen via those vertical striations], it smells really strongly of ammonia."

After sniffs all the way around (the verdict was mixed), Richardson pulled out his honey bear, a plastic cartoon-bear-shaped squeeze bottle that contained water instead of honey. Selecting a biscuit-sized clod from the surface of the soil he had just dug up, Richardson informed us that we were going to perform an experiment—we were going to measure how long it took Goven's cattle-massaged soil to absorb a drop of water. Printz stood with his digital stopwatch at the ready as Richardson squeezed a drop of water out of the honey bear. The drop touched the soil biscuit and was absorbed so quickly it was as if it had vanished. It went directly from being a droplet hanging on the pointy tip of the honey bear's spout to a wet spot on the soil biscuit. Printz, who had started the stopwatch on command, was unable to stop it as quickly as the event had happened. The test was over in the same instant that it started.

PHOTO: COURTESY OF DR. JIM RICHARDSON

Next we drove across the road to a part of the Goven Ranch that had been included in the Federal Conservation Reserve Program (CRP). This land had been restricted from grazing and the raising of crops for fifteen years as part of a government program to leave some agricultural lands fallow. The program was intended to let some lands recover from farming as it also helped keep farm prices up by keeping farm production down. The land within the CRP exclosure was flatter than the grazed land we had used for our experiment across the road, but we selected a site as comparable as possible. Halfway between a high point and a low point in a field, Richardson pulled out his sharpshooter and started to dig. At least he tried to start digging. Bouncing up and down on his shovel as if it were a pogo stick, he finally managed to jackhammer a hole a few inches deep. He then showed us that the soil

According to Dr. Richardson's studies, Goven has been able to increase the ability of his land to absorb water more than six times… Then he showed us the rich black color of the soil. "That's the carbon," Richardson said. "It's an echo of the Pleistocene."

The biscuit was selected, the drop was squeezed, the stopwatch started. As the droplet perched on the CRP soil biscuit, the first second passed on the watch's digital display. Then two, three, four seconds—the drop was still there, pearl-like and perfect, glinting in the sun.

here was a light gray rather than the rich black we had seen in the pasture. He also showed us that there were fewer roots in what soil he could dig up, and that the land here was striated horizontally rather than vertically. When it came time for the sniff test, again it smelled like dirt to me. Richardson and Goven, however, detected a strong ammonia smell, "Phew! You don't smell that?"

Time again for the honey bear. The biscuit was selected, the drop was squeezed, the stopwatch started. As the droplet perched on the CRP soil biscuit, the first second passed on the watch's digital display. Then two, three, four seconds—the drop was still there, pearl-like and perfect, glinting in the sun. We all continued to wait, slightly hunched, watching closely. One minute. Two minutes. Still there. Still no change.

At two and a half minutes, the drop was still intact, and the soil beneath it perfectly dry. At this point, we all became bored and aborted the test. Some of us speculated that the drop would evaporate before it would be absorbed.

This surprising difference in infiltration rates between the rested and used parts of Goven's ranch has a number of consequences. For one thing, because the grazed part of Goven's land comes so close to achieving his goal of capturing every raindrop where it falls and routing it into the soil, it frequently experiences almost no runoff after a rain. Meanwhile, Goven's neighbors' potholes and stock-watering ponds or "tanks" fill immediately from surface runoff. Goven's fill a few days later from the bottom up, from water that has come through, rather than over, the soil.

And because more water stays at home to nourish Goven's grass, the cattle that graze his land now leave behind as much forage for wildlife as they used to find when Goven first moved them onto a pasture.

"My pastures used to produce 2,000 to 2,500 pounds of grass per acre and my cows used to eat all but about 1,000 to 1,500 pounds of that. Now, when I take the cows off, I leave about 2,000 to 2,500 pounds," Goven says. And while Goven's cattle now leave more grass on a pasture than once grew there, they produce more beef.

Perhaps the most notable benefit of Goven's mutualistic management, however, is reminiscent of those days of the great bison herds. When American settlers first came to the Great Plains, they found those plains underlaid by a deep, black soil of unsurpassed richness. Subjected to the plow, this soil produced an unprecedented bounty, but it became obvious over time that if withdrawals from this ecological "bank account" continued without some new deposits, it would gradually deteriorate.

Until recently, no one knew how to make those deposits, at least not on the scale at which they were originally created. The black soils were considered to be an act of God, or more properly, of Mother Nature, and therefore it would take God or nature to restore them. Jim Richardson, however, has suggested a different way.

"The grazing technique Gene Goven uses has a long history here on the northern Great Plains," says Richardson. "In fact, it was developed by Mother Nature herself." Richardson explains that Goven's technique of concentrating cattle and moving them across the land as if they were a nomadic herd duplicates the way bison once grazed these prairies, recreating a process that replenishes the Great Plains' magnificent soils. When Goven's cattle bite a grass plant, they remove some of the tissue the plant uses to receive energy from the sun to fuel the production of food and growth. The plant then finds itself unable to support as much tissue mass as it could before it was bitten. When this happens, the plant reabsorbs some of the material from its roots in order to create enough light-receiving tissue to extend it high enough to expose it to the sun again. As a result, those roots die back and are sloughed off into the soil.

"It's sort of like drawing on a reserve account to make an investment and reap a return later," says Richardson. Once the plant has retrenched and produced enough new, chlorophyll-containing tissue to catch the sun, it can continue on its way to making seeds and completing its annual cycle—if there is no cow or bison there to bite it again. As a result of this process, the plant contributes the organic material in those roots, a main component of which is carbon, to the soil. Do this over and over again for tens of thousands of years, bison bite after bison bite, retrench and regrowth after retrench and regrowth (lub-dub, lub-dub…), and you have prairie soils that become black with sequestered carbon.

Norm Lowe (my partner on those EcoResults! restorations) calls this kind of grazing "pulsed grazing." The name makes a great image. When grazing is used as Gene Goven and some other members of the Lost Tribe use it, as a form of CPR, it can pump life back into ecosystems that are all but dead. This sort of pulsed grazing is the technique the Tiptons used to get native plants to grow on that heap-leach pad. It's the method the ranchers of the Rio Verde Ranch used to produce the grassy meadow that stopped the flash flood. And here in North Dakota it is the method Gene Goven used to restore a soil that traces its lineage back to the Pleistocene.

This has value beyond mere restoration. Pete Jackson has said an acre of healthy

Goven's technique of concentrating cattle and moving them across the land as if they were a nomadic herd duplicates the way bison once grazed these prairies, recreating a process that replenishes the Great Plains' magnificent soils.

grassland continuously removes more carbon from the atmosphere, and releases more oxygen into it, than an acre of rainforest. Atmospheric carbon, in the form of carbon dioxide, is the main cause of global warming.

There are a number of reasons grasslands can be more effective at sequestering carbon than a forest. For one thing, an acre of grassland includes a huge amount of functioning, photosynthetic green tissue and not a lot of nonphotosynthetic limbs and stems. Second, grass plants have as much as 90 percent of their biomass underground while trees have 90 percent of their tissue above ground. In other words, there's a lot more to those grasslands than meets the eye. Furthermore, a healthy grassland, i.e. one with a pulse, pumps carbon from the atmosphere into the soil via lub-dub grazing while a forest, especially a rainforest, harbors quite a bit of rot and decomposition, thus actually releasing carbon dioxide.

Why not just do this sort of restoration grazing with bison? you might ask; create a Buffalo Commons, as some have suggested, and let the animal that created the original grassland symbiosis of the Great Plains recreate it? A friend of mine once said that a herd of bison without a band of Blackfeet chasing it is the same as a bunch of cows. In other words, bison turned loose to roam as they please and eat as they choose will have much the same

If you graze bison the way those animals would have grazed with a band of Blackfeet shadowing them, you get the same beneficial effect. Duane Lamers shadows a herd of bison on the 777 ranch in South Dakota.

effect as a bunch of cattle doing the same. They will eat the tasty, nutritious plants over and over again until they overgraze them to death, and they will pass over the weeds until that is pretty much all that is left. I've seen this happen in a number of cases. Why would it not happen?

On the other hand, if you graze bison the way Gene Goven and the Tiptons and most of the rest of the Lost Tribe graze their cattle, the way those animals would have grazed with a band of Blackfeet shadowing them, you get the same beneficial effect as the cattle. Several well-managed ranches, such as the /// in South Dakota, provide examples of this. Some say bison are more beneficial. Some don't. The plants don't seem to care.

The fact is any one of a number of animals can serve this purpose. In Arizona I've seen this kind of restoration achieved by goats and on the Deseret Ranch in Utah by elk. On a ranch near my home in Flagstaff, I have even seen a class of sixth graders get respectable results stomping and trampling hay mulch into land that looked very much like the Drake Exclosure. On the Work Family Ranch near San Miguel, California, the Works—George, Elaine, Kelly, Ben, and Dawson—raise forage for wild boar that are considered a plague by just about everyone else in the state. Hunters then harvest the pigs and help support the ranch. The disturbance the pigs cause rooting for acorns under the ranch's oaks plants whatever acorns the pigs don't eat. Some of these then sprout into little oaks. George Work speculates that the wild pigs perform a task, as rooters and oak planters, that grizzly bears once filled.

One of the things Work has become known for is leading field trips onto his ranch to point out the boar-oak symbiosis. He also enjoys pointing out the water troughs he has designed which are accessible to rabbits, lizards, mice, and snakes as well as cows and boars. Traditional metal, cement, or plastic tub-style troughs are inaccessible to many species and can be a death trap for some. Work's "drinkers" are designed to be self-cleaning so the boars can't foul them. They have a central channel too narrow for a cow to step into or a boar to lay in. That channel includes a special little escape ramp so the tiniest lizards and mice can avoid being trapped and drowned. These inventive troughs as well as Work's ability to turn a nuisance into an asset (the boars) helped to gain him the National Cattlemen's Beef Association Environmental Stewardship Award for 2004. ■

Pete Jackson has said an acre of healthy grassland continuously removes more carbon from the atmosphere, and releases more oxygen into it, than an acre of rainforest. Atmospheric carbon, in the form of carbon dioxide, is the main cause of global warming.

Near Mina, Nevada

— CHAPTER SIX —

LEARNING ON THE FRINGE

ECCENTRIC GENIUSES IN A GHOST TOWN ▪ WATER RISES TO LIFE

STEPPING ON THE SPONGE ▪ TERRA PRETA REVISITED

IT'S UP TO THE BUGS ▪ PLEISTOCENE PARK — IF WE BUILD IT,

WILL THEY COME?

I am fascinated with the idea of "life making the conditions for life available to life," especially where it involves humans. One could say the purpose of this book is to establish that humans actually can be a part of this sort of relationship with nature and to make us better able to recognize the instances in which we are. The reason for so doing, of course, is to enable us to participate more fully in those relationships once we've realized we are part of them.

One of the most off-the-wall examples, and therefore one of the most paradigm-stretching learning experiences, I have encountered of life making the conditions for life available to life happened at the hands of some of my favorite teachers, the Tiptons. It took place in one of the most unlikely locations for higher learning that I know of—the near-ghost town of Mina in western Nevada, or as Al Medina calls it, "la Mina" (the Mine), where the Tiptons live in their Pink Panther bus.

Stephen J. Gould—perhaps the most famous writer on evolution other than Charles Darwin—tells us that evolution happens on the fringes in the ecotones. It happens in places where species have to cope with circumstances that are a stretch for them and that pose new challenges they must deal with in order to survive. Mina is such a place. It is certainly on the fringe, and it certainly requires adaptability in order to live there. Mina is about as near a ghost town as a town can be and still be alive. It has one motel, one restaurant, one place to buy a burger, and a couple of places to buy beer where you can sit down and drink it. The one substantial brick building in town is collapsing around its For Sale sign. A couple of gas stations sell a few groceries. Both have a "coffee nook."

At one of these one-stop-shoppers I asked the lady behind the cash register if I should pay before I pumped gas.

"Go ahead and pump," she said. "Anybody who has a truck like that has to have a job." I wasn't sure my three-year-old pickup, which is relatively free of dents and has doors that are all the same color as the rest of the body, was all that impressive, but after Tom Bean and I bought gas and enough groceries for a couple of lunches and breakfasts, she threw in the ice for free. (Tom and I had opted to camp rather than listen to another night of revelry in the megaphone hallway of the town's lone motel.)

Mina's most "going concern" is located at a polite distance just south of town. It is a brothel that advertises itself on one of those blinking arrow signs on wheels with a programmable message scrolling across the light bulb array. "OPEN—NEW GIRLS— ATM," the sign winks. I found out about the public-service aspect of this establishment when I tried to pay my bill at the motel with a credit card. "Whoa," I was told. "We can't take plastic here. We've barely got telephones. The only ATM in town is back down the road, at the brothel."

"I'm just here to use the ATM," I said when a young woman answered my ring at the door.

Scattered around town and off into the desert, in various mobile homes and other structures, some of which require a close look to tell if they're occupied or abandoned, live a number of what one person described as "eccentric geniuses."

Scattered around town and off into the desert, in various mobile homes and other structures, some of which require a close look to tell if they're occupied or abandoned, live a number of what one person described as "eccentric geniuses." Some of them make up Mina U.'s research faculty. Many of these graduates of the school of hard knocks are eccentric enough to require this kind of setting to pursue their genius because it probably wouldn't be tolerated in more conventional communities. One of the members of the research faculty told me he's working on a more effective way to extract metals, including gold, from ore that would otherwise be too poor to mine. "I have to develop the chemicals used in the process in temperatures that get above fifteen hundred degrees," he said. "Even in a full fire suit that gets warm."

I try to imagine any structure in or near Mina that could withstand that kind of heat without exploding in flames. I can't.

The people of the Pink Panther, Tony and Jerrie Tipton, fit right into this setting. That scares me in some of my more sane moments, when I realize that I have kept track of what they've been doing since I first met them in the mid-1990s. Having been made more tolerant of academic diversity by my periodic visits to the Mina campus of Learning-on-the-Fringe U., and by the successes I have seen the Tiptons achieve, I no longer dismiss anything I hear from them, no matter how crazy it seems. (And I'm quicker to give other people the benefit of the doubt, too.) But when Tony Tipton told me he could bring more water to the surface in that dry Nevada desert by putting cows on the land, I was sure he had gone too far.

"Rain follows the plow." The slogan that created the Great Dust Bowl still stands as one of the most striking examples of how much trouble wishful thinking can get you into when you apply it to the environment. "Water rises to the cow" sounds way too close to that for me.

But Tony and Jerrie don't just stand there and talk when they spring something like this on you, they load you into the pickup and take you out and show you. Actually, as I understand the story, I was with Tony the day he first came to this realization.

It was in 1995. I was helping the Tiptons herd a couple hundred cattle more than a hundred miles across Nevada. The Tiptons were taking the cows from what was then their ranch near Austin in the center of the state to the BLM grazing allotment on Cedar Mountain near Mina that is now the center of their operations. I remember the day we reached our destination. In the morning we gathered the cattle, which had scattered a bit, and began moving them toward the narrow notch that formed both the entrance to and the outlet from a place called the Douglas Basin. It was a glorious day. The rabbitbrush was in bloom. The sky was a polarized blue. After several days on horseback, I was finally feeling comfortable in the saddle. For the first time, the horse and I were able to move as a unit. As we jumped, ran, and spun behind the cattle, pushing them through the rabbitbrush, golden petals filled the air. It was as if the horse and I were swimming through a sea of gold.

Tony noticed that day that the trickle of water flowing out of the basin increased significantly as we drove the cattle into it. From that he came up with the theory that the added weight of the cattle brought the water to the surface. Having made that observation, he began carrying an auger with him out on the range. Whenever he and Jerrie would bring their cattle into a new area, Tony would auger a hole and measure the distance down to water or at least to where the dirt was wet. After the cattle had been there for a while, he would measure it again. More often than not, he reports the water was closer to the surface after the cattle had been there for a while than it was when they first came.

Other people to whom I have mentioned this—range managers, scientists—have described this hypothesis as "nuts." If that's the case, one expert said, New York City should

Whenever he and Jerrie would bring their cattle into a new area, Tony would auger a hole and measure the distance down to water or at least to where the dirt was wet.

On the right-of-way side of the fence the grass was brown. On the BLM side it was green. Same species of grass. Same type of soil.

have water squirting out of it thousands of feet into the air (because the buildings are so heavy). But when I asked some construction workers if they had ever experienced anything like this, they said it was a common phenomenon for them. They said that frequently, when they park heavy equipment on an area, it brings sufficient water to the surface that they have to bring in pumps to keep the place from becoming a quagmire. New York isn't squirting water thousands of feet into the air because the water has been squeezed out gradually, as the materials and equipment were brought to the site as the buildings were constructed.

Tony's hypothesis made sense out of an earlier experience I'd had on another field trip to the outer limits of Mina. On that field trip Tony showed us a fence line that separated BLM rangeland from a highway right-of-way. On the right-of-way side of the fence the grass was brown. On the BLM side it was green. Same species of grass. Same type of soil. Tony told us that he and Jerrie had held their cattle on the BLM side of that fence for a couple of days a few weeks before our visit. He said when they did that, they found there was water here. To demonstrate, he used his boot heel to scrape a trench about six inches deep into the dirt on both sides of the fence. The dirt was moist just a few inches under the surface in both cases. When the cattle had been here, their weight had squeezed the water out of the dirt, so some of it came to the surface and became available to the salt grass plants that lived there. This caused those plants to green up and begin to grow. On the other side of the fence the grass had remained brown and dormant. That's the same thing that had happened in the Douglas Basin, I thought now in retrospect. That's why more water flowed out when the cows went in.

And what's so weird about that? I wondered. What's so weird about living beings on the surface of the desert having the ability to make what water is present more available to them? Actually, when you think about it, the opposite of that seems more unlikely—that life wouldn't have a way to access that water.

In the way of grazing used by the Tiptons (and by nature, too), the animals come onto the land in large numbers, in a herd, forcing subsurface water toward the surface where it becomes available to life. And then the Tiptons, or some other members of the Lost Tribe, or human or animal predators—the herders of nature—move the animals off the land. When their weight is removed from the sponge, the land is ready to absorb more water when it rains or snows, and then it all happens again, and again, and lub-dub…lub-dub…lub-dub…

For all those who say this is too good to be true, the Tiptons have a very good response. They say you don't have to believe them; you can ask nature. That's what they've done. And they can show you where she has answered, "Yes."

TERRA PRETA ON THE RANGE

In "1491" when William Woods told Charles Mann that humans had created the self-renewing Amazonian soil anthropologists had named terra preta, and Mann said he was so amazed he "almost dropped the phone," Woods suggested to Mann that "Scientists should study the microorganisms in terra preta to find out how they work. And, if they succeeded," Woods added, "[M]aybe some version of Amazonian dark earth could be used to improve the vast expanses of bad soil that cripple agriculture in Africa—a final gift from the people who brought us tomatoes, corn, and the immense grasslands of the Great Plains."

When Woods said those words, it's a fairly good bet he wasn't referring to the research faculty at Learning-on-the-Fringe U. in Mina. That may be, however, where the discovery he hoped for has been made. In the Nevada desert, Tony and Jerrie Tipton have also located a type of soil that is capable of self-regeneration and able to resist the depletion of nutrients. And they, too, have concluded that this discovery could be used to improve the vast expanses of degraded soil that cripple agriculture and ecosystem restoration in the American West. No doubt it could be useful in Africa as well.

During one of my periodic calls to find out what was up at Fringe U., Jerrie told me that she and Tony were coming to believe that the plants growing at any particular place may be dictated to a great degree by the composition of the microbial community in the soil of that place.

"The bugs," as Jerrie called them, "may have more to do with what's growing there than anything else." If that's true, Jerrie explained, it may tell us why some of these areas have changed from grasslands to monocultures of juniper trees (as has been the case on the Drake).

"If that's the case, and you could figure out how it works," I said, paraphrasing Mann, "you could solve one of the biggest environmental problems facing the West."

Since European society arrived, one of the biggest problems on large dry ecosystems in the West has been the Dr. Jekyll and Mr. Hyde phenomenon of native plants, usually woody plants like junipers, becoming invaders and acting like aliens. These Jekylls-become-

Since European society arrived, one of the biggest problems on large dry ecosystems in the West has been the Dr. Jekyll and Mr. Hyde phenomenon of native plants, usually woody plants like junipers, becoming invaders and acting like aliens.

Hydes have transformed lands from savannas supporting diversities of plants and animals into monocultures that then begin to lose soil and become virtual wastelands, sometimes eroding to bedrock. Throughout the West juniper trees, sagebrush, creosote, rabbitbrush, and other woody natives have undergone this freaky transformation and subjected millions of acres to this sort of desertification. Uncounted millions of dollars, probably billions, have been spent burning, plowing, bulldozing, spraying, and chainsawing these mild-mannered plants turned monsters back into submission. One of the more extreme tactics has involved uprooting them with marine anchor chains dragged across the landscape by large bulldozers. This in turn has destroyed cultural sites, killed and displaced wildlife, uprooted valuable plants, caused pollution, contributed to global warming, inspired millions of dollars worth of lawsuits, and taken money from other, more worthwhile projects, while the invaders have, in almost every case, begun regrowing before the bulldozer was out of sight.

If the Tiptons are right, and these invasions are just a symptom of a change in the subsurface soil community, and if that soil community could be changed back to what it was before the invasion, making the soil less hospitable to the invaders and more hospitable to desired plants, such as perennial grasses, this would indeed be a momentous discovery. The icing on this cake would be if this transformation could be brought about by animals rather than bulldozers, as was the case with those trincheritas I described earlier.

To make sure the Tiptons were on the right track, I called Dr. Elaine Ingham, president of Soil Food Web, Inc., an organization that analyzes soil for land managers and recommends actions to achieve specific results. When I asked her if areas dominated by invasive exotics (or invasive natives) have different soil microbial communities than areas that support healthy populations of native perennials, her answer was yes. And when I asked if someone could use the "if you build it, they will come" approach to create a soil that was hospitable to natives and inhospitable to exotics, again the answer was yes.

After my initial conversation with the Tiptons about the value of soil microbes, they told me that, as they drove around their ranch, when they saw a healthy individual of some native plant species they wanted to restore to some other area of their ranch, they would scrape some of the accumulated organic material from around the plant's base and toss it into an empty fifty-gallon oil drum in the back of their pickup. This compost, they believed, was rich in the material, including soil microbes and the like, that made that plant so vigorous. When they had collected a significant amount of this compost, they would add water and molasses to feed "the bugs" (microbes) in it, add a small aquarium heater and aerator, and let the mixture "cook" until it formed a frothing culture of native microbes. (Organic gardeners call this a "compost tea.") Then they would spray this mixture on the soil in places where they were trying to restore the same sort of plant community as the one that had been the source of the "bug juice." In some cases they skipped the water treatment, accumulated a bunch of the duff, sifted out the twigs, rocks, and other chunks, and added the material to the seed mix they broadcast through their seed spreader.

Simpler still, they merely added molasses to the hay they fed to their cattle and let the animals feed the soil microbes in situ with the molasses they didn't eat but tromped into the soil. The fertilizer supplied by their animals' excrement supplemented the meal.

When the Tiptons saw a healthy individual of some native plant species they wanted to restore to some other area of their ranch, they would scrape some of the accumulated organic material from around the plant's base and toss it into an empty fifty-gallon oil drum in the back of their pickup.

Restoring microbial diversity to the tens of millions of acres of rangeland soils from which it has disappeared is not just a daunting job, it is an impossible one without the aid of animals. Just as large grazing animals serve as an essential instrument in the formation of trincheritas on a scale broad enough to restore function to rangeland watersheds, the Tiptons' animals play an essential part in all the techniques they employ to restore the subsurface soil community. Their animals help incorporate into the soil the liquid bug juice they spray on its surface. Same for the screened dry stuff and the molasses-in-situ bug food. Where the Tiptons don't provide an inoculant, the animals scrape the microbe-rich duff from under the plants and tromp that into the soil.

PHOTO: DAN DAGGET

Simpler still, the Tiptons merely added molasses to the hay they fed to their cattle and let the animals feed the soil microbes in situ with the molasses they didn't eat but tromped into the soil. The fertilizer supplied by their animals' excrement supplemented the meal.

If the Tiptons (and Elaine Ingham) are right that there is a chicken-and-egg relationship between what lives in the soil and what grows on it, and the Tiptons are right that grazing animals have a mutualistic relationship with the microbial community associated with grassland soils, we can gain from this a more complete explanation of why the area outside the fence at the Drake Exclosure was more diverse and more covered with plants than the area inside. Most likely, it was because the microbial community outside was more plentiful, more diverse, and more appropriate to a grassland. In fact, during our field trip, Al Medina pointed out that this was indeed the case. Al told us that under the trees of the juniper monoculture within the Drake the soil community was made up almost entirely of fungi, and in the bare areas between the trees it was exclusively bacteria. Outside the exclosure the soil was inhabited by a more diverse community of bacteria and fungi.

When I asked later how that came to be, and what mechanism made it happen, he replied, "It's that lub-dub grazing you talk about. When the animals pump organic material into the soil, they are feeding the microbial community. When that stops happening, well, the Drake shows us what happens."

Medina also provided an observation that supported the Tiptons' contention that disturbance provided by grazing animals can promote diversity in the soil community. He reminded me that there were some areas in the Drake on which there was more grass than others. Those areas, he explained, were where trees had been cut down, or had even been bulldozed, to free up water for other plants. While the bulldozers were knocking down trees, he explained, they mixed the fungi-rich duff under them into the fungi-poor soil. "More plants grew where the bulldozer hooves went," he said.

The importance of various components of the soil microbial community to certain plants can't be overemphasized. Certain plants, for instance, can only absorb water and nutrients via mycorrhizae—symbiotic relationships with fungi. Because of this, some species of orchid were so difficult to germinate that the techniques to do so were closely guarded secrets until a French botanist named Noel Bernard discovered that the penetration of the seed by a mycorrhizal process was what made germination possible.

Describing how important these symbioses are to plants, Peter Corning writes in his book *Nature's Magic,* "An estimated 80 percent of all land plants depend on the services provided by…the more than 5,000 species of mycorrhizae that augment the plant's own root system." Mycorrhizae play a key role in "the transfer of phosphorous and other minerals to the plant's roots" and make it easier for the plant to absorb water and resist pathogens. "In fact," writes Corning, "seedlings planted in soils where nutrients are abundantly available will still grow poorly or not at all without their symbiotic 'fungus roots.'"

OUT OF AFRICA

The Tiptons have had considerable success using animals to reverse the kind of desertification represented by the Drake and other areas reduced to monocultures of woody invasives. The practices they use, as we have said, are based on the model of natural grazing. These practices were first described by Alan Savory, who had been a game warden in Zimbabwe. Savory noticed that even though the grasslands and savannas of Zimbabwe were grazed by huge herds of wildebeest and other ungulates, those grasslands persisted, even thrived, under that heavy impact and concentrated use. Savory noticed that nature's grazers kept moving and rarely stayed in one place long enough to regraze the plants as they recovered. And as they moved, those animals created what I called "trincheritas," enriched the soil, pruned the plants, cycled the duff, and opened the ground-level growth centers of the grass plants to the sun. Savory then noticed that when domesticated animals were grazed in the same way, they had the same effect.

Inspired by this observation, and convinced that the only way to live effectively on a planet inhabited by systems or "wholes" was to be aware of these sorts of relationships and to manage in harmony with them, Savory devised a management model called Holistic Management. The Tiptons have adapted this model, emphasizing two of its more revolutionary aspects. First is the use of animals to restore and sustain a whole suite of mutualistic relationships involving humans, grazers, and grasslands. Second is the use of collaboration among the human players to make sure there is a diverse enough collection of "receivers"—humans with differing values—to make sure their team doesn't miss any of the feedback the land is giving them.

In spite of their efforts to include as broad a diversity as possible in their projects, and regardless of their success on the land, the Tiptons continue to have the problems I have described communicating their message through the Leave-It-Alone blinders worn by so many of us who form the contemporary environmental community. Showing dog photos to cat fanatics doesn't come close to describing it.

You can imagine how frustrating that can be, especially to a couple of people for whom this is their life's work. Because of this, the Tiptons spend a lot of time wondering how to make their case effectively, how to toss it over the Leave-It-Alone monolith, or beam it through, or have some scientist publish it on the other side. And so they keep upping the ante with ever more difficult projects in the hopes that they can finally do something that is too big or too outrageous to ignore.

The most outrageous one they have come up with yet is a real humdinger. It would involve actually recreating one of those Edenic icons the Leave-It-Alone movement uses

The Tiptons spend a lot of time wondering how to make their case effectively, how to toss it over the Leave-It-Alone monolith, or beam it through, or have some scientist publish it on the other side.

(inaccurately) to prove its effectiveness. They would create it in the flesh, alive, functioning—a sort of Pleistocene Park that people could visit and walk around in and see how it works.

"I want to restore Teels Marsh to what it was ten thousand years ago," Tony told me in one of his ante-upping moods. At first I thought he was joking, then I realized he wasn't. Mann said Indians often worked on such a grand scale that the scope of their ambition can be hard to grasp. The same can be said, with a little tongue in cheek, about the Tiptons.

These days Teels Marsh is anything but a marsh. It is a large salt flat at the center of a 300,000-plus-acre mountain-rimmed watershed.

U.S. Geological Survey data and maps indicate that in the early 1870s Teels Marsh was a wetland of standing water and marsh vegetation surrounded by grasslands and savannas. One of the current residents of the nearby ghost town of Marietta can recall ducks being hunted on the marsh as recently as the 1940s. Local residents maintain that until the early 1960s large herds of mule deer wintered in the area.

Today, there is no marsh vegetation here in spite of the fact that there has been more precipitation in the last forty years than in the previous forty. The watershed is so desertified that what rain does fall is shed into the basin, where it rapidly evaporates, leaving behind a crust of the salty minerals it leached out of the surrounding soils. Where there was marginal grass as recently as the early 1980s, grasses are now nearly nonexistent. Current production of grasses both native and introduced has been measured at from zero to fifty pounds of dry matter per acre. In contrast, one of the Tiptons' reclaimed mine sites has produced as much as six thousand pounds per acre.

These days Teels Marsh is anything but a marsh. It is a large salt flat at the center of a 300,000-plus-acre mountain-rimmed watershed.

To restore Teels Marsh the Tiptons would rehabilitate about 100,000 acres of the 300,000-acre watershed, impacting about 20,000 acres per year. To do this, they would use the sort of lub-dub grazing we have talked about earlier, moving large herds of animals onto and off the land and letting it rest in between. They would do this on a scale large enough to impact this significant watershed by means of a process they have named "The Movable Feast."

The feast would be created by borrowing a large number of animals from a feedlot

The Tiptons tried their approach on part of the Teels Marsh watershed. The top photo shows their results. The bottom photo shows the same relative area without their treatment.

and turning them loose onto the range where they would be transformed from a source of pollution into an instrument of restoration. Instead of standing confined on piles of their own excrement, the cattle would be able to move across the landscape, breathing the fresh air and enjoying a degree of freedom that is as different from a feedlot as it is possible to be. And while they were enjoying that freedom, they would eat and fertilize, plant the native seeds the Tiptons broadcast in front of them, feed the soil bugs, create trincheritas, and get more plants to grow, which in turn would route more water into the soil. With the water in the soil instead of on the surface, where it evaporates almost as quickly as it falls, the basin would become more moist, and the marsh would be reborn.

"I figure if we can get the soil to absorb three or four times as much water as it has been absorbing, that's the same as tripling or even quadrupling the rainfall," calculates Tony Tipton. "With a watershed in as bad shape as this one is, that shouldn't be all that hard to do."

When you come right down to it, this sounds like a pretty saleable project. It certainly has a number of saleable aspects: throwing open the doors of the feedlots and allowing the animals to range free; transforming those feedlot cattle from environmental and moral liabilities into tools of restoration; restoring the mutualism between humans, our partner/prey animals, and the environment; and creating spillover benefits the way a coral reef does. Those sound like goals most environmentally concerned people would be interested in supporting, but there's another aspect of this project that should make it a no-brainer.

Teels Marsh is located one mountain range east of the Owens Valley, the valley from which Los Angeles collected and rerouted water to nourish its explosive growth in the early twentieth century. As late as 1913, Owens Lake fluctuated between 20 and 45 feet deep. Steamboats hauled ore across it. The dewatering of the Owens Valley watershed has changed that catastrophically, transforming the valley from an oasis to an arid basin. Storms of salt and dust have become common. The U.S. Geological Service has called the Owens Valley a "spectacular example" of human-caused ecosystem desiccation, describing the dry lake bed in the valley as probably the largest single source of very fine dust pollution in the United States. With much of its means of replenishment removed, the water level of Mono Lake, which is also located in the valley, has dropped precipitously and become a bumper-sticker cause among environmentalists.

The Tiptons estimate the budget for the Teels Marsh project to be about $2.5 million to get the project up and running—$5 million for a complete restoration. The latter figure would include extensive monitoring and scientific studies. Either of those totals would be a bargain if the project could shed light on how to solve some of the problems of the Owens Valley and Mono Lake.

Funding the Teels Marsh project would probably not be a problem, at least not an insurmountable one. Getting it approved is a different matter. The project plans have been on the desk of the BLM for eight years and counting. What's the holdup?—some of the same roadblocks the spikedace and the southwestern willow flycatcher efforts have experienced. As this book goes to the printer, however, late-breaking news suggests the logjam may be beginning to soften. ■

By borrowing a large number of animals from a feedlot and turning them loose onto the range, they would be transformed from a source of pollution into an instrument of restoration.

Dawson Work on the Work Family Ranch, San Miguel, California

CHAPTER SEVEN

RETURN OF THE NATIVES

A WORLD OF RELATIONSHIPS, NOT OF THINGS

MAKING HOME HOME AGAIN ■ LUB-DUBBING A REFUGE ■ GETTING

NATIVES TO INVADE INVASIVES ■ LEARNING IN THE DEAD ZONE

T he science of quantum physics may sound like an odd discipline to turn to for insights on how to solve some of the more resistant environmental problems of the day, but on one problem at least it has proved to be fertile ground. Here's how. Scientists working to identify the most elemental unit of matter were discovering smaller and smaller particles until they suddenly came to a point where there were no particles. In fact, there were no things. There were only relationships. For some, the implication was clear—we live in a world of relationships, not of things.

While this may sound like another hifalutin scientific irrelevance, it has a lot of ramifications for life as we know it. For our purposes here, it sheds an important light on one of the most aggressively pursued campaigns of modern environmentalism—the campaign to restore native plants to ecosystems from which they have been extirpated, or in which they have become much less common than they once were.

Restoring those plants is usually treated as a replacement of things—of replanting the plants (or returning the animals) to where they used to be. Once we've done that, we consider that place to be restored—to be as it used to be or, at least, to be more like it used to be than it was when those plants weren't there.

The intent here, of course, is to reverse the damage done by humans. The natives we work so hard to return are ones that have become more rare or extinct because we've made them that way. I've characterized the idea that we can heal the land by leaving it alone as an effort to fool nature into thinking we're not here. Restoration as a matter of putting things back the way they were takes that subterfuge a step further. By putting things back the way they were, by replanting native plants where they used to be, we're trying to con nature into thinking that we never were here, that all those human-caused impacts were just a bad dream. This thing-based version of restoration assumes that nature will take up where she left off and everything will be as if we had never messed it up. It assumes that we can put Humpty Dumpty back together again. That we truly can wash our hands of what we have done. That we can turn back the clock.

A philosopher once said, "You can't step into the same river twice." It has been my experience that many of the places to which we would restore these natives have changed so much that our "natives" are no longer native to them. In fact, in many instances, these purported "natives" can no longer even survive in the places to which they are supposedly uniquely adapted—the places where evolution has supposedly shaped them to fit better than any other plant or animal.

What if the place to which some plant or animal is supposed to be native has had its effective rainfall reduced to a small fraction of what it once was, even though roughly the same amount continues to fall from the clouds? And what if the soil microbial community of that place has changed so dramatically or has been diminished so drastically that it favors a completely different kind of plant?

Does it make sense to plant natives in an area so transformed and expect them to survive? Even to thrive? Should we be surprised if a totally different cast of players, things we call noxious weeds, move into that place and prosper? Perhaps these exotics are native to the new conditions. How smart would we be if we went into those areas and poisoned the plants that now are able to live there under these new conditions and expect plants and animals that lived there under totally different conditions to somehow turn back the clock and make the place the way it used to be?

Consider our old friend, the Drake Exclosure. Which of the plants that once lived in the Drake are native to it as it exists now? When those "natives" are planted in the exclosure they die. When their seeds blow onto the exclosure, as they regularly do, they fail to germinate.

The activity that supposedly made the Drake alien to its natives—overuse—has been removed. The Drake is no longer overused. It's not used at all. According to the dominant environmental paradigm, it should become home again to its natives. But the natives haven't returned. This phenomenon is being repeated all across the West. More and more areas that are being "protected" or have been transformed by other forms of alien management are being invaded by noxious weeds. If they're lucky, that is. Some, like the Drake, won't even grow weeds. Perhaps these ecosystems and the plants that were once native to them are trying to tell us something.

One thing they could be telling us is that the alien solution—resetting the table the way it was and hoping we can fool nature into thinking we've never been here—doesn't work. They could be telling us that being native is a matter of relationships. They could even be telling us something about our role in those relationships.

If we try to restore a native cactus that relies on a bat to pollinate it into an area where there are no longer any of those bats, and the cactus doesn't make it, should we be surprised? If we try to reintroduce an orchid that relies on certain mycorrhizae to enable it to germinate, shouldn't we try to reintroduce the mycorrhizae, too?

In a world of relationships, just replacing things isn't enough. If we want these

These ecosystems and the plants that were once native to them could be telling us that the alien solution— resetting the table the way it was and hoping we can fool nature into thinking we've never been here—doesn't work.

restorations to work, we have to restore the relationships these natives rely on as well. That means we have to determine what these relationships are. How can we do that? We can ask the authority most capable of giving us an accurate answer—the native itself, and the ecosystem to which we would restore it. How do you do that? You try something and see if it works. If it works, you know you've restored a synergy. If it doesn't work…

In North Dakota, Gene Goven is successfully restoring a native—the black soil of the Great Plains—by restoring the relationship between grazing animals, the plants they graze, and the rich living soil that supported both. Managing his cattle to graze in a way similar to the way bison once grazed those prairies, Goven was able to have them function the same way bison once functioned, as a massive pump, pumping carbon into the soil to increase its richness and enable it to grow sufficient grass to support huge numbers of bison.

Restoring these same sorts of relationship has worked in other places as well. On the Audubon National Wildlife Refuge (NWR) near Coleharbor, North Dakota, wildlife biologist Craig Hultberg is returning native grasses to the refuge by restoring relationships involving grazing animals, fire, and the prairie. As a result of Hultberg's efforts, not only are nonnative grasses such as smooth brome and crested wheatgrass giving way to native big bluestem, green needle grass, and sideoats gramma, but birds are prospering as well.

On a visit to the refuge in August 2003, Hultberg offered to take Tom Bean and me on a tour of the refuge and show us the results of what he was doing.

On the Audubon National Wildlife Refuge near Coleharbor, North Dakota, wildlife biologist Craig Hultberg is returning native grasses to the refuge by restoring relationships involving grazing animals, fire, and the prairie.

"We're getting natives to invade invasives," Hultberg continued. "In most places, it's the other way around."

"I'll tell you the way I got started," said Hultberg as he drove. "I wanted to get rid of Canada thistle, and I heard about what Gene Goven was doing. It sounded good. I looked at Gene's pasture. At the time, I was spending much of my time spraying [with pesticides]."

Using a program of pulsed grazing and fire alternated with letting the land and the plants recover—a program inspired at least to a degree by what he saw at Gene Goven's ranch—Hultberg says, nonnatives are being replaced with natives.

"When I started," Hultberg continued, "the refuge was 25 percent Canada thistle. Now it's maybe 1 percent.

"Twenty years ago they asked me to find some big bluestem, and I couldn't find it. Now I can't not find it."

Hultberg stopped the car at what seemed to be a random point. "I get a kick out of this when I see it happen," he said as he stepped out of the car.

"This is idle," he said, pointing to the side of the road away from Lake Audubon, the most prominent physical feature of the refuge. "That's [smooth] brome, crested wheat, and Kentucky blue." (All are nonnatives.)

"Over on the other side of the road, look at the diversity. See the big bluestem coming in here? There's some little blue [little bluestem], too, and there's some green needle grass. All of these are natives. We're getting natives to invade invasives," Hultberg continued. "In most places, it's the other way around."

As he walked through the restored area, he continued. "We grazed this a year ago, seeded it while we were grazing, and then we burned it. If you burn it and leave it, you've got the bad stuff, the invasive tame stuff, coming in. You've got to graze it the next year. Fire opens it up. Grazing closes it up. You can't use burning [alone] to take rangeland to excellent condition."

As we continued our tour through this area that once had been crisscrossed by herds of millions of bison, we came to an area that was in the process of being restored. The scene here reminded me that functional relationships aren't always pretty. I've become accustomed to sights like this after years of working with people like the Tiptons, but I can imagine what most bird watchers would think if they came upon something like this at a wildlife refuge. Without having talked to Hultberg or someone familiar with his approach and its success, I'm sure they would be absolutely apoplectic. They would be convinced a disaster was underway.

The land looks hammered, stomped, overgrazed. Cattails around a prairie pothole near the road are ragged, bent, broken, cropped, and chewed. The cows have trampled well-used paths through the barrier the cattails had formed around the edge of the pothole. Areas of the shoreline are trampled and littered with cattail stumps. Manure is plentiful.

Hultberg tells us that he uses animals to remove some of the cattails because they're so prolific they form nearly impenetrable barriers around the potholes. This makes the water of the pothole virtually inaccessible to some species and replaces the "edge" habitat, where the mix of water, cattails, and grasses serves wildlife so well, with a monoculture of cattails. In some cases these aggressive water-loving plants invade the potholes so thoroughly that they obliterate them, making them useless to many of their old beneficiaries. On our tour we see that some potholes that have suffered this fate have been reopened by burning and grazing.

As for the people who inevitably question, or complain about, Hultberg's methods, he has a response as atypical as his restoration methods. He invites them to go out onto an area that has recently been treated with cattle and walk across it with him. If they agree, and they usually do, he keeps walking so his companions can't keep talking. He does this, he says, in order to get them to listen. He leads them across land that hasn't been grazed onto land that has been grazed as hard as at that pothole I just described.

"I walk them right into the 'Dead Zone,'" he says. "And then I ask them, 'Did you hear the difference? Did you hear the bugs, the birds, and stuff?' When I ask them that, they get the point."

Back at refuge headquarters, Craig tells us what he feels has been the ultimate compliment he has received about the job he is doing. "A woman came here who was taking pictures of wildlife refuges around the West," he said. "On other refuges she took pictures of the wildlife. Here, she took a picture of our prairie. When I saw her picture, I cheered inside."

Other people are using this synergistic relationship between grazing animals and the land to make the land once again home to its natives. Not too far from the Audubon NWR, near Underwood, North Dakota, a large coal surface mine, the Falkirk Mine, has managed its grazing program to successfully enable native grasses to recolonize areas where nonnative grasses were seeded after mining.

Within the city limits of Bismarck, North Dakota, Gabe Brown is actually redeeming land out of the Conservation Reserve Program (CRP), where it has been converted almost entirely to nonnative grasses (smooth brome and crested wheatgrass), and restoring it to native prairie. In doing so, he loses the subsidy that comes with having land in the CRP.

"I walk them right into the 'Dead Zone,'" he says. "And then I ask them, 'Did you hear the difference? Did you hear the bugs, the birds, and stuff?' When I ask them that, they get the point."

"I have to pay more for that land because it has an assured income," Brown says. "So I start out in the hole, but I restore it to native prairie, and the beef I raise pays for it. That's a pretty good deal for the people who value native prairie." Brown told me this as we watched his cattle move across one of his pastures. And then he added, "Imagine how much more native prairie we could restore if we were paid to do it."

NATIVE CALIFORNIANS

In California the mutualism between humans, ungulates, and grasslands has been facilitating the return of some of that state's most picturesque natives.

In a 1973 article published in *Fremontia*, the journal of the California Native Plant Society, James W. Griffin wrote: "Where are the young trees under the big oaks? One can drive through literally tens of thousands of acres and not see a single valley oak sapling." Griffin said it was possible for the persistent searcher to find a few young trees but continued that the situation was clear that, in 1973, valley oaks were not being replaced on large portions of the California savanna.

In a more recent article (1990), Griffin wrote: "Throughout California major areas of oak woodland remain; but locating healthy, mature, or young regenerating oak stands unthreatened by agricultural or urban development is becoming increasingly difficult."

Valley oaks have been described as one of California's signature trees. Their graceful, spreading profile, dark green in contrast to an undulating landscape of lighter green or golden grasses, has been called as characteristic of California as its towering redwoods. An image I have of a milk-chocolate-brown doe, her coat slick and gleaming, standing in grass

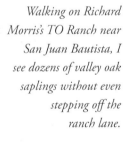

Walking on Richard Morris's TO Ranch near San Juan Bautista, I see dozens of valley oak saplings without even stepping off the ranch lane.

almost to her belly while browsing the leaves of one of these oaks will last as long as I'm alive. This lack of a new generation of these Hobbitesque living sculptures becomes more serious as the older ones die or are removed for whatever reason and are not replaced. Among the causes to which this decrease in California's oaks had been attributed is livestock grazing.

Walking on Richard Morris's TO Ranch near San Juan Bautista, I see dozens of valley oak saplings without even stepping off the ranch lane. At other places on the ranch, Richard's son, Joe, who manages the TO, shows me other valley oak saplings, ranging from knee high to taller than I am. At one point, he kneels down and parts the leaf litter to show me a tiny oak sprout—the ranch is producing seedlings, too. All of these valley oaks are growing in areas that are regularly grazed in an approach employed to restore the ranch's native plant community.

As we continue our tour of the TO, Joe shows me examples of native perennial grasses sharing the hillsides with the oaks. He combs the grass blades through his fingers as he names them. Creeping wild rye, purple needle grass, blue wild rye. In some places, there are so many we lose count. This is not the usual state of affairs. In California, native perennial grasses have been displaced by nonnatives, mostly annuals, on a scale that seems impossible. In some places, the landscape is completely covered by these invaders. These plants were brought here from the Mediterranean and Eurasia by Spanish colonials and others. Some were imported intentionally. Others hitchhiked as a pollutant among seeds or feed. Some have formidable names—ripgut, medusahead. All are effective colonizers, as effective as the people who brought them here.

The TO is small, only a couple of hundred acres, so Joe Morris has taken on the management of a couple other ranches and grazing "places" in order to have them all add up to a living for his family. Among these are parts of two state parks. In each of these other areas Morris pursues the same goals as he does on the TO—making the land healthier, more diverse, with more stuff growing on it and less erosion removing soil from it. He was contracted to graze the parks because of his reputation as a manager. Park management thought that he would do less damage. Now he's trying to convince them that he can actually make the place better.

Joe shows me other valley oak saplings taller than I am. He combs the grass blades through his fingers as he names them. Creeping wild rye, purple needle grass, blue wild rye. In some places, there are so many we lose count.

"Sometimes I think I'm making headway, and sometimes I don't," Morris tells me as we view an area where he has used cattle to try to make the land inhospitable to invading medusahead. Joe used hay to entice his cattle to crowd onto the area and trample organic material into the soil. This, he hopes, will make the land home to its natives once again.

As Tom takes photos, Joe and I try to project the results of this effort. Success depends on a number of things, but the most important is always rain. Not only does enough rain have to come, but it has to come at the right time. The true results of this project won't fully be "in" until a year later, after a full growing season. Right now, however, it has a little of that "Dead Zone" look to it that Craig Hultberg referred to. It looks like a place where too many cattle have been for too long a time. That means Morris has his work cut out for him reassuring park administrators that what he has done here is something that can be described as restoration rather than devastation.

TAKE A COW AND CALL ME IN THE MORNING

The message here may sound like the answer to everything is grazing—that cows are the cure, no matter what the problem. Though these stories may strike you that way,

"Sometimes I think I'm making headway, and sometimes I don't," Morris tells me as we view an area where he has used cattle to try to make the land inhospitable to invading medusahead.

this misinterprets the message they contain. What Joe Morris is doing to make the land he manages home to its natives again is slowing the flow of water off the land and increasing its flow into the land. He's increasing the amount of carbon the land is sequestering and enhancing the diversity of the soil's microbial community. He's preparing the ground for seeds to grow. Cows are merely the instrument he uses to do this.

One could, I suppose, use machines to do the same thing, or urban volunteers, or whatever, but machines or volunteers can't do it as well as animals can. Why? Evolution has shaped animals to do these jobs just as it has shaped the jobs to be done by animals. Evolution has shaped the cow's mouth to be broad, like a lawn mower, so cows can eat grass effectively, just as it has shaped the deer's mouth to be narrow, so it can be an effective browser of shrubs. It has shaped these animals' feet to till the soil, encouraging the growth of the plants on which they feed, and designed the function of their guts to feed the soil and complete the cycle. In addition, evolution or nature (whatever you choose to call it) has designed these animals to be able to decide what is right to eat and when to eat it, and to go where it is best to go when it is best to go there. How hard would it be to design a machine to do that? Who would pay the huge development costs it would take? And why bother when we already have creatures that do it so effectively?

PHOTO: DAN DAGGET

Using plants, animals, and the land in the way that Joe Morris uses them embodies the most basic relationship in nature. Living things relate to one another by using one another. Animals use plants as food and shelter and the like, and plants use animals to prune them, remove their waste, distribute and plant their seeds, and so forth. Use is the transaction by means of which the business of life is conducted. It is the means by which life makes the conditions for life available to life.

The early Gardeners of Eden facilitated this interaction just as Joe Morris does. Early human hunters not only hunted as individuals stalking individual animals or as small bands working to bring down a large critter such as a mammoth or grizzly, they also hunted in groups or packs by herding. And as they did, they facilitated the lub-dub movement of the animals across the land. Throughout the West there are remnants of brush and rock corrals into which ancient hunters would herd animals to trap them. Evidence suggests that some of these sites have been used for thousands of years. Judging from petroglyphs, bones, and other evidence, and from the oral histories of members of various tribes, these ancient herding devices were used to capture antelope, elk, deer, bighorn sheep, caribou, and even bison. Some tribes still participate in roundups of jackrabbits.

In other words, the method of moving animals across the land used by Joe Morris and other members of the Lost Tribe works so well to make the land home to its natives again because the method itself is native. Recreating it recreates the net of relationships that made it possible for the plants and animals we call native to live there in the first place. ■

One could, I suppose, use machines to do the same thing, or urban volunteers... but machines or volunteers can't do it as well as animals can. Why? Evolution has shaped animals to do these jobs just as it has shaped the jobs to be done by animals.

Fire in the Arizona Forest

— CHAPTER EIGHT —

EDEN IN FLAMES

BUBBLE CITIES AND SPACE STATIONS ▪ THE MYTH OF NATURAL FIRE
FIRE OPENS THE DOOR ▪ FIRE THAT'S WARM AND FUZZY
CONTROLLED UNTIL THE FIRST MATCH ▪ HYDROPHOBIC SOILS

In the same way that people throughout the West are looking for a way to make it rain more, there are probably more of us wondering how to make it burn less, or at least to burn less uncontrollably. Wildfire—catastrophic, lethal, capricious, a natural force stoppable only by other natural forces—has become the most pressing environmental problem facing the American West. In 2002, wildfire burned 2,929,028 acres in the West. That's a landmass roughly the size of Connecticut. That disastrous wildfire season included the largest wildfires in recorded history in Arizona and Colorado—roughly half a million acres in each case. In 2003, in southern California over 750,000 acres were burned in fifteen large fires that destroyed more than 3,400 homes and over 1,100 other buildings and killed twenty people. Included among these conflagrations was the largest fire in California history, the 272,000-acre Cedar Fire.

That's the bad news. The even worse news is that, before our culture arrived on the scene and started putting fires out, the fire frequency in some areas of the West has been determined to be as short as a fire every two to ten years. These areas are accustomed to burning. They have evolved to burn. They want to burn. They try to burn.

The best way to truly appreciate this is to lie in bed at night, as I have, knowing the forest around your neighborhood is tinder dry as you listen to the rapid-fire cannon-shot thundering of a dry lightning storm. If you spent the evening watching TV news reports of people evacuating their homes ahead of towering flames, sleep can be a rare commodity.

In spite of the need of these areas to burn, modern fire-suppression practices have kept some of them from doing so for the greater part of a century. As those years have counted off, the materials that would have fueled those fires have accumulated. With some of the highest lightning-strike frequencies in the world, with people flicking cigarettes out their car windows, with campers making campfires, government agencies starting controlled burns that sometimes get out of control, and vandals actually trying to start fires, the question is not *if* those accumulations of fuels will burn. It is *when*.

The answer our environmental and land-management communities have settled on to deal with this situation has been to abandon the policy of suppression and facilitate the return of "natural" fire. If disrupting the frequency of natural fire caused the problem, this theory goes, restoring natural fire will solve it.

This approach, however, faces a couple of significant obstacles and suffers from a colossal inaccuracy that should be getting familiar to you by now. The first obstacle is that fuel loads have become so large in the West that when fires do happen there is a significant chance that they will become big fires. Big fires not only threaten human communities (and frequently deliver on that threat), but they can wreak great damage on the environment as well. Hot fires fueled by bloated accumulations of fuel have been known to sterilize the soil so thoroughly that even noxious weeds won't grow there, at least for a while. This in turn promotes erosion and other problems that can keep the land from ever doing anything that could be termed "recovery."

The second obstacle to the return of natural fire derives from the fact that so many western communities are very close to large areas of forest, and so many of us have built homes in remote areas surrounded by trees. For these reasons, mentioning the word "fire" in the western countryside is almost like shouting it in a crowded theater. It makes a lot of people very nervous.

To deal with these problems, two major strategies have been suggested. One would have us harden or fireproof the areas around our communities and let the fires burn in the backcountry. If you build your home in the backcountry, proponents of this method say, well, you made your choice and you'll have to take your chances. Left to burn, the story goes, nature will burn herself back to a natural state, or as close as is possible given the way humans have changed these areas. Fire will then return to its natural character—more frequent, smaller, cooler fires that are easier for the ecosystem to recover from. Once this happens, the story goes, it will even destroy fewer remote homes.

This remedy is based on the Leave-It-Alone premise that nature existed in a state of "balance" before humans disrupted it, a state of balance that included smaller, benign fires rather than large catastrophic ones.

The other strategy (supported by most of the professional land-management community, including government agencies) would use chainsaws, bulldozers, controlled burns, and even herbicides to return the West's forests and savannas to the more open character we're now fairly sure they had before fire suppression began. Once the ecosystem is restored to conditions that are described as "presettlement" or "presuppression," this approach also assumes natural fire would keep it that way and prevent fuels from rebuilding. According to this theory, some areas may have to undergo this treatment a few times before natural fire would take over and sustain them. In spite of that, proponents are confident that this return to benign fire would eventually happen because they assume the land kept itself in balance before humans messed it up, and so it'll do the same once we un-mess it.

This strategy is another example of what I've been calling an "alien" solution. It assumes that we (humans) had nothing to do with the workings of things when they did work, and so putting everything back the way it was before we got here (presettlement conditions) would

The second obstacle to the return of natural fire derives from the fact that so many western communities are very close to large areas of forest, and so many of us have built homes in remote areas surrounded by trees.

fool nature into thinking that we've never been here, and… You get the picture.

The first strategy, the "fireproof the areas around our communities and let the backcountry burn" strategy, is an alien solution, too, but in a more interesting way.

Although fireproofing the areas around our communities and allowing the backcountry to burn is posed as the most natural strategy (because it would leave the most land alone), it is the most alien of all. In fact, this strategy takes my point about "acting like aliens" from metaphor to matter of fact. What this strategy would do is turn our communities into bubble cities, earthly space stations similar to the Biosphere II that was constructed near Tucson, Arizona, in the 1980s. Within these bubbles—to which we are already retreating via the policies others call protection and I call abandonment—the environment would be managed closely and protected from fire. Outside the bubble, the rest of the world would be abandoned to whatever happens to it—to what Leave-It-Alone advocates call nature, and I call the great environmental gamble. As we've learned from the lesson of the Drake Exclosure, this would result in a world of space stations surrounded by a world of Drakes. Such a world could still serve as combination art exhibit, zoo, cathedral, and adventure park within which we could still act as sightseers, worshipers, caretakers, and joyriders, because we can do those things perfectly well, maybe even better, in a wasteland.

I call the return to a natural-fire regime a gamble for the simple reason that it never existed, at least within any time frame that is relevant to us. For that reason, we can't know what trying to recreate it will produce. This is the colossal inaccuracy I referred to earlier. The situation in which fires were more frequent and smaller and more manageable that natural-fire advocates promise to recreate by returning to a natural-fire regime, wasn't created or sustained by nature or natural fire. It was, in fact, created and sustained by the Gardeners of Eden, who applied fire as a developed, intentional strategy of management.

"The study of a pure [natural] fire regime, so dear to American ecologists is a fantasy," writes fire historian Stephen Pyne in his University of Washington Press book *Fire in America: A Cultural History of Wildland and Rural Fire*. "Mankind is the primary source of fire in the world."

Pyne tells us that American Indians used fire for much more than the familiar uses of heat, cooking, light, and firing ceramics. They used it to aid in the cultivation and harvest of grasses, berries, and nuts. They burned areas near their camps to drive off mosquitos and flies. They used fire to kill broad areas of forest so those trees could be used for firewood, or they burned the trees to ash so they would serve as a fertilizer for slash-and-burn agriculture. They set fire to the litter on the forest floor to roast the fallen cones of sugar pines, turning the seeds into a delicacy. They used fire to smoke pandora moths from the trees, so they could pick them off the ground and eat them. They used fire to prevent fire, burning areas around their villages so those areas wouldn't provide fuel to carry a fire (that they had most likely started) into the village, and they burned camp areas when they moved on to clean them for next year's use. They even used fire as a rainmaker, "burning miles of mountain landscape," as Pyne puts it, in the "delusion" that this would bring rain. Going beyond utility, they used fire for purposes of ceremony and celebration. Lewis and Clark reported Indians torching tall fir trees for the entertainment provided when these trees exploded like Roman candles.

American Indians used fire…to aid in the cultivation and harvest of grasses, berries, and nuts. They burned areas near their camps to drive off mosquitos and flies.

The most extensive use of fire by those ancient Gardeners, however, was to create habitat amenable to the animals they relied on for food and other uses (those bumper crops of elk, deer, and bison Mann referred to in "1491"). Pyne writes, "In the general absence of domesticated livestock, meat had to come from hunting, and through fire Indians maintained … the grassland or forest-grass ecotone…that proved so productive of game."

Indians used fire to drive animals from one place to another, to surround them while hunting them, and to attract them to the fresh regrowth that sprouts after a fire. In fact, Indians used fire so effectively and so aggressively to expand the grasslands that sustained the animals they hunted that, according to Pyne, they extended the grasslands outward from their central core on the Great Plains into Wisconsin, Michigan, and Minnesota, east through Illinois, Indiana, Ohio, and Kentucky, and south into central Alabama and Mississippi.

Another measure of the extent of the use of fire as a land-management tool by the Indians is the frequency with which they applied it. Pyne says grassland areas were typically burned every other year.

"If you doubt this story," Aldo Leopold wrote in *A Sand County Almanac* three-quarters of a century in advance of Pyne's book, "go count the rings on any set of stumps of any ridge woodlot in southwest Wisconsin. All the trees except the oldest veterans date back to the 1850s and 1860s, and this was when fires ceased on the prairies."

That much burning over millennia of Indian management created an ecosystem for which burning every few years became as natural as plants shedding their leaves in winter. The Indians were able to live in that fire-adapted land by adapting their lifestyle to it. They became nomads, scheduling their moves to harmonize with their burning. They may have danced with wolves, but they certainly danced with fire.

We live in the remnants of this fire-ecosystem, so we have to deal with fire. We have no choice. If we don't deal with it, it will deal with us. We're not going to become nomads. We can't just protect the land and expect everything to be all right—we're learning in terms too hot to deny that approach doesn't work. So we're left to come up with another solution.

Uncomfortable situations like this usually create learning opportunities. This one creates a number of them. I've already pointed out that it gives us one more opportunity to learn that another of those Leave-It-Alone icons—the natural-fire regime—was created, not by leaving the land alone, but by humans. I don't think we can learn this lesson too many times.

Beyond that, the wildfire crisis presents perhaps the best opportunity yet for us to learn that the health of the land is a matter of its condition, not of the degree to which it is protected. It's easy to ignore this lesson when it comes from flycatchers, spikedace, or watersheds—who listens to little birds, fishes, or bare dirt—but when the wake-up call comes from fire, it's a lot harder to ignore. Remember the guy who said, "If you leave, no matter what happens, it will be natural and therefore good." It's a whole lot harder to make that statement if the consequence is, "It'll burn my house and a lot of other peoples' houses and a bunch of habitat and animals and…."

Fire also presents perhaps the best opportunity yet for us to learn that what we do to benefit ourselves can also benefit nature. Catastrophic wildfire can burn so hot it can sterilize

Indians used fire to drive animals from one place to another, to surround them while hunting them, and to attract them to the fresh regrowth that sprouts after a fire.

the soil, retarding the ability of plants to regrow in those areas. This, in turn, can cause calamitous erosion which can remove soils to bedrock in some areas. Catastrophic wildfire can destroy huge areas of habitat, severely impacting wildlife populations and threatening endangered species. When we make nature less likely to burn in order to protect our homes, we also protect it from these impacts.

Add to all of the above the fact that people consider fire a mostly natural phenomenon, and the result is that communities using fire to protect themselves from wildfire face less environmental opposition than they do in other instances of managing nature to benefit themselves. This, in turn, has lowered opposition to using fire to deal with other environmental problems. For example, fire is now being used to combat noxious weeds, to fight insect infestations, to restore grasslands that have been overrun by a variety of invasive species, and to return biodiversity to areas that have converted to woody monocultures. This isn't really new. Fire has been used for these "other purposes" for some time now. What's new is the broader acceptance these other uses enjoy because of the acceptance of using fire to prevent wildfire.

By opening the door to a broader acceptance of managing the environment to our benefit, using fire to prevent catastrophic wildfire has lowered

Fire is being used to combat weeds, to fight insect infestations, to restore grasslands that have been overrun by a variety of invasive species, and to return biodiversity to areas that have converted to woody monocultures.

opposition to using other methods to prevent wildfire and even to solve problems that have nothing to do with fire. For instance, grazing livestock on public lands, especially on lands that haven't been grazed for a while, invariably attracts opposition. When grazing is used to reduce the danger of catastrophic wildfire, however, the reaction is different, at least to a degree.

GETTING FIRE'S GOAT

After the 2002 Rodeo-Chediski Fire in Arizona burned nearly a half-million acres, destroyed over 400 homes, and forced 32,000 people to flee ahead of its flames, I was sorting through the photos I have taken of functional ecosystems over the years. I was trying to determine if any of those photos held a hint of how to deal with the West's fire problems. And then I remembered a photo I took of the aftermath of a large wildfire in Montana. The photo showed that a fire that started on the Montana Game Range, a wildlife preserve near Cascade, had stopped when it reached the border of Chase Hibbard's Sieben Ranch. After a little digging, I found the photo. It showed that the fire had stopped on a straight line— the ranch boundary. Fires don't usually stop on straight lines unless they have help, so why did this one?

The easiest conclusion was the one most people would leap to when they learned that one side of this line was grazed by livestock and the other wasn't. Most people would

A fire that started on the Montana Game Range, a wildlife preserve near Cascade, had stopped when it reached the border of Chase Hibbard's Sieben Ranch.

PHOTO: DAN DAGGET

conclude that the livestock-grazed side didn't burn because there was nothing there to burn because the cows ate it all.

A closer look at the photo showed that definitely wasn't true. The ranch side of the fence wasn't a wasteland, and it couldn't have been a wasteland in the year it burned, because it had trees on it—big trees, healthy trees, trees that had been there a while. The only difference I could see between the two sides was that on the ranch side the trees hadn't burned and on the preserve side they had. Why didn't the trees burn on the ranch side? When I looked at other photos I had taken of the Sieben Ranch, the most striking feature of those photos was how green they were. The grasses of the ranch were positively iridescent. Grass stays green longer when it has more moisture available to it (and more moisture in it). The fence line contrast on the Sieben Ranch displayed the same difference as the fence line contrast at the Drake Exclosure. The ranch side of the Drake fence looked more moist because it was. The ranch side of that Montana fence looked more moist (i.e., it wasn't burnt) because it was more moist as well.

That brought back all those earlier realizations about effective rainfall, trincheritas, more plant stems, and such. And it made me aware of another benefit of making the land more effective at absorbing water—doing so makes the plant community growing on that land less flammable.

The opposite of this is also true. Plants that are more dry are more flammable. This dryness, I assume, can result from less rain falling from the clouds or from less effective rainfall entering the ecosystem. If a forest or grassland is absorbing only a small percentage of the precipitation that is falling on it, the plants growing there can be experiencing drought in a normal rainfall year, even in a wetter-than-normal year, and be more prone to fire as a result.

We are, of course, talking about probabilities here. About shades, not absolutes. No doubt there was a time that year when the grasses on Chase Hibbard's side of the fence were dry enough to burn, too, but the number of days when that was the case were fewer than the days the preserve was capable of burning. We certainly know there was at least one day on which the preserve was more flammable than the ranch (the day of the fire). And even on those days when the Hibbard side of the fence would burn, it is my bet that it would burn less vigorously than the other side because of residual moisture its plants might contain. An increase in atmospheric humidity can make a fire burn less vigorously. It seems logical that an increase in the humidity within a plant and the soil around it would have the same effect. In fact, during the 2004 fire season, California fire departments recommended keeping plants growing near houses hydrated in order to make them less likely to carry a fire to residences.

So, the question arises: Could our mutualistic relationship with animals, and its ability to increase the moisture-storing capacity of ecosystems, lower the fire danger in the West? An answer is offered by a project that happened on the Prescott National Forest in central Arizona.

After the disastrous fire season of 2002, the Prescott National Forest (PNF) contracted a fellow to bring in a herd of goats to reduce a dangerous fuel overload on a brushy hillside on the windward side of the city of Prescott. Using a controlled burn was rejected because the area was too close to town for the sake of safety and clean air. These are common problems

Could our mutualistic relationship with animals, and its ability to increase the moisture-storing capacity of ecosystems, lower the fire danger in the West?

The goats did what goats do: ate and chewed and trampled. When they were finished, the brushy hillside was changed significantly.

when dealing with fire and controlled burns in the increasingly urban West. The goat option was chosen because the PNF was looking for an opportunity to test tools that didn't create these problems.

This project was one of those feel-good collaborations that produced winners all around. The goats were recruited on the nearby Navajo Reservation, which was in the throes of a crushing drought. Plenty of animals on the "rez" were in need of a meal that year, and Navajo goat owners were pleased to be offered an opportunity to send their animals to Prescott to eat brush and get fat while they performed a public service. Those goatherds were also pleased because, while their animals were eating a firebreak around Prescott, their home pastures could rest and recover from a drought that had lasted for the better part of a decade. For those reasons, the target of six hundred hungry goats was reached easily.

The goats did what goats do: ate and chewed and trampled. When they were finished, the brushy hillside was changed significantly. Plants that had been touching and would carry a fire easily now had space between them. The limbs and leaves that grew back after they were browsed were green and moist and less flammable than what had been there before.

Of course, the goats achieved this without releasing large amounts of pollution into the air and without getting out of control and consuming any subdivisions or killing anyone. Afterward, they went back to their reservation homes fat and presumably happy. Presumably the Prescott National Forest and the citizens of Prescott were happy, too. Another group that benefited from the project was the wildlife that got to eat the greener, more moist, more nutritious food that grew after the goats had grazed, much as it would have grown after a fire.

Projects like this show us that animals can be used to do some of the things we have just re-realized that fire can do. We cannot only fight fire with fire. We can fight it with goats. And we can use goats to fight noxious weeds, and restore grasslands, and restore and sustain wildlife habitat, and increase water yield from dysfunctional watersheds. Goats can do so many of the same things as fire, we could call them "fire with hooves" or fire that's warm and fuzzy instead of hot and dangerous. Actually, other animals can serve these purposes, too. In Georgia, sheep are eating kudzu—"the vine that ate the South." On the Deseret Ranch in Utah, elk are helping to restore a desert grassland, and we know what the Tiptons can do with cows.

Why is that valuable? There's a saying about a controlled burn: that it's "controlled" until someone strikes the first match. Animals are a lot less dangerous than the most well-

Another group that benefited from the project was the wildlife that got to eat the greener, more moist, more nutritious food that grew after the goats had grazed, much as it would have grown after a fire.

PHOTO: DAN DAGGET

controlled burn. Also, burning some hillside to reduce an accumulated fuel load, whether it's done naturally or not, doesn't mean it won't burn again, and very soon. While I was watching television coverage of the destructive fires in southern California in 2003, one man who was interviewed said he had picked the site for his new house (which had just burned) because the area had burned "five or six years ago." For that reason, he considered the location to be safe, at least for some time into the future. Considering the fire frequencies Pyne talks about—every two years in some cases—the site was already overdue.

Conducting controlled burns over extensive areas of the West every few years to keep down the fire danger would be outlandishly dangerous, expensive, and polluting. Reducing fire danger with animals every few years creates no such problems. It could be planned a lot easier, controlled a lot better, and it would have fewer negative and more positive side effects than a burn. To boot, it would produce food and, in the case of the Navajo goats, mohair and Navajo rugs and Navajo culture as byproducts. It could even make money instead of costing money.

There's one more way I haven't mentioned in which humans working with animals can offer the West relief from the damage caused by fire. They can help heal its aftermath. Fire can bake the surface of the soil into a ceramic-like shell that repels water. Soil to which this has happened is called "hydrophobic." When rain falls on this water-repellant surface, it runs off, coursing downslope, gaining mass and power until it tears through the shell. Then, with access to the fire-dried dust under that shell, it erodes like crazy. This is why, after a fire, rainfall events that would normally be harmless can cause mud slides and flash floods, and big rains can cause catastrophes.

Hydrophobic soils not only repel water, they also shed seeds and resist penetration by the roots of seed sprouts. Scientists and land restorers report being able to scoop up hard hats full of native seeds that were expensive to buy and expensive to spread from gullies and streambeds in burned areas after a rain.

After a fire, wild animals often return to an area while stumps and logs are still smoldering. They come to lick the ashes for trace minerals and roll in them to coat themselves with a dusting of ash that repels fleas, ticks, and lice. They eat the succulent green shoots that sprout almost immediately after a fire. As they move, they break the hydrophobic crust, creating a means for the soil to absorb water, so less of it flows over the soil and away, ripping and tearing as it goes.

Stripped of their herders by the transformation of humans from pack hunters to sport hunters, "wild" animals rarely herd up in sufficient numbers to do this job well. But domesticated animals do—when they get the chance. U.S. government policy is to bar livestock from burned areas on public lands for at least two years, in some cases more. Accordingly, when the animals are allowed back onto the land, all the damage has usually been done. When animals are used to rehabilitate burned land, the results are more like what animals have been able to do on land denuded by mining.

Because so many of us in the West live so close to a potential holocaust, the threat of catastrophic wildfire has done more than perhaps anything else to shake the free pass the Leave-It-Alone assumption has enjoyed for the last century. This crisis has caused us to realize

When animals are used to rehabilitate burned land, the results are more like what animals have been able to do on land denuded by mining.

that we do have an interest in managing the environment beyond transforming it into a combination adventure park and cathedral. There's another way in which following our own self-interest can reconnect us to the land, a way that also sheds some light on how we can finance the re-gardening of Eden. ■

Doe and Connie Hatfield, Brothers, Oregon

— CHAPTER NINE —

THE ECONOMICS
OF EDEN

THE CURRENCY OF MUTUALISM ▪ ORGANIC, NATURAL, GRASS-FED, AND
PASTURE-RAISED ▪ AN EPIPHANY FOR AN INVESTIGATIVE JOURNALIST
THE CONFLICT ECONOMY ▪ THE ADVANTAGES OF USING MORE LAND

Food was the heart of the economy that produced the Edens of pre-Columbian North America. It was the currency that paid for all the burning, herding/hunting, and gathering that produced those icons of pristine nature. Food paid for the nomadic lifestyle that management by fire and hunting made necessary. Food also funded the production of the byproducts of that management—the healthy watersheds produced by the trincheras and trincheritas maintained by humans and the animals they hunted, the healthy soils and healthy plants sustained by the lub-dub grazing and browsing of animals hunted by herding. It even paid for the carbon sequestration that the Indians presumably didn't need because they didn't drive SUVs and cause air pollution. Then again, in light of all the burning they did, maybe they did need it.

Some contemporary Gardeners are working to revive this long-lived economy, to once again use food as the currency to fund the mutualism of humans, animals, and ecosystems. By doing so, they would also restore food to its traditional function as a source of feedback that proves whether that mutualism is working or not.

Two of the pioneers in this effort are Doc and Connie Hatfield of Brothers, Oregon. In 1986 Doc and Connie and thirteen other ranchers put together a cooperative named Oregon Country Beef (OCB). Originally, the purpose of this co-op was to help family ranches survive in an economy fraught with hazards. At the time, attrition was high among small producers for a number of reasons. For one thing, beef was being sold as a commodity or generic product, which meant it brought lowest-common-denominator prices. Add to this the high costs of environmental compliance that had been raised to a maximum by people committed to removing ranchers from the land (you know, the only thing you can do is leave), and you have a situation that creates the ideal conditions for consolidation. Costs were high, prices were low, and the big fish were eating the little fish.

113

While OCB was struggling to survive, it was contacted by a Japanese company that wanted to market its products. The Japanese have a reputation for paying a lot of attention to what they eat. Having a close relationship to a producer would enable them to influence the quality of what they were consuming. This relationship paid off for OCB, too, in more ways than cash flow.

"We learned an awful lot about how to run a business from the Japanese," said Connie.

Due to the success this relationship yielded, OCB quickly came to be looked up to as one of the most successful examples of selling beef as something other than a commodity. OCB products were something for which people would pay more in order to get more: food that was free of additives, high in nutrition, and produced by caring people in a way that was good for the land. It was food that helped sustain open space and the element of diversity that rural agricultural families add to our culture. Those were goals many Americans could feel good about supporting.

Oregon Country Beef sells beef that is labeled "natural," defining that term the way their main customer, the Whole Foods supermarket chain, defines it. Whole Foods defines natural beef as beef that is raised with no growth hormones, no antibiotics, and no animal byproducts (so it can't be infected with mad-cow disease).

When the Japanese economy crashed, OCB experienced a setback. Thanks to a growing concern for healthy food in the U.S., however, it recovered and resumed its growth. Recent concern about the food supply, fueled by a number of crises, have bolstered that growth. A few months after I visited the Hatfield Ranch in 2003, I called and asked Doc how things were going. During the time that had passed since my visit, the first cow in the United States had been diagnosed with bovine spongiform encephalopathy, and the nation had been wracked by a "mad-cow" scare. Against the backdrop of that heightened concern, the rate of annual growth of demand for Oregon Country Beef had increased from 27 percent to 42 percent, and the cooperative had added sixteen ranches, growing from forty ranches to fifty-six. To find enough ranches to meet the new demand, OCB had to go outside Oregon into Idaho, Washington, and northern California. When I called again a couple of months later, I learned that OCB had grown to seventy ranches.

Oregon Country Beef sells beef that is labeled "natural," defining that term the way their main customer, the Whole Foods supermarket chain, defines it. Whole Foods defines natural beef as beef that is raised with no growth hormones, no antibiotics, and no animal byproducts (so it can't be infected with mad-cow disease). Whole Foods says it also works to ensure that its products are produced by "farmers and ranchers who care about the animals and the environment in which they live."

When Tom Bean and I visited the Hatfields, we decided that the most appropriate place to meet them would be in a market that offered their products for sale. Doc chose the Newport Avenue Market in Bend, Oregon.

At the market, when customers visiting the meat counter learned that Doc and Connie were two of the ranchers who produce Oregon Country Beef, we had no trouble getting them to talk about the product and what they thought about it. All said they were extremely glad that they could feel it was okay to eat meat again. One trim and fit woman, who said she had recently moved to Bend from San Francisco, enthused to Doc and Connie: "I've been a vegetarian for thirteen years. I'm a runner. I'm very concerned about what I put in my body. I've only been eating meat for three months, and I'm so glad you're doing this." Employees of the market told us the same thing.

At the market, when customers visiting the meat counter learned that Doc and Connie were two of the ranchers who produce Oregon Country Beef, we had no trouble getting them to talk about the product and what they thought about it.

Several people, both customers and staff, said Oregon Country Beef was the only kind of meat they ate in spite of the fact that it cost more than commodity meat.

The manager of the market, Spike Bement, said he had been concerned about this cost differential early on, when he first started selling Oregon Country Beef, but when a chain grocery store opened nearby he decided to "bite the bullet" and exclusively sell OCB. At the time, he said, the store's meat department was failing.

"It was the best move we could have made," he declared.

A while later, at the Pine Country Restaurant, people at a number of tables extended their compliments to Doc and Connie for what the ranchers of Oregon Country Beef were doing—and for the quality of the meat they were producing. A few invited the Hatfields to their table.

Whenever I was part of those conversations, I tried to steer some of them toward the environment. In each case, the response was brief, and the conversation went right back to health issues. It was as if these people were thinking that, having established that the Hatfields were concerned enough about health—their health—to raise healthful food, then they were probably concerned enough about the land to be doing a good job with that, too. And that was good enough for them.

Not everyone feels that way. Some people object to raising cattle on the land, no matter how it's done, especially on public land. The Hatfields' ranch and other ranches in the OCB cooperative are typical of ranches in the West in that much of the land their animals graze is federal land on which they lease grazing rights. To anyone who doubts that the Hatfields are taking care of this land, Doc and Connie have responded in a couple of ways. First, they and the other members of Oregon Country Beef have adopted and published a set of "Grazewell Principles" that they follow in their management of the land. And they have made it clear that anyone who doubts the quality of their management can come out to the ranch and look for themselves. They'll even show them around.

The few times people have taken them up on this offer have become stories that get repeated, as in, "Remember the guy who...."

In one instance, a member of the Audubon Society accepted the Hatfields' tour offer. According to Connie, after visiting the ranch, he praised them for some practices they were using that benefited birds in a way they weren't even aware of.

"He talked about how we were benefiting neotropical migrants by the way we handled the slash from our juniper cuttings," Connie explained. "I'd never heard the name 'neotropical migrant.' I didn't know what he was talking about, but I know now."

During an antigrazing demonstration in Bend, the Hatfields invited some of the demonstrators out to their ranch to see how they treated the land. Connie said that none of the people they made the offer to took them up on it.

"They said they didn't need to see," said Connie.

The most widely recognized person to accept the Hatfields' tour offer was Ed Marston, publisher (at the time) of the *High Country News*, one of the most respected environmental journals in the country. Marston came to the ranch as an investigative reporter interested mostly in the Hatfields' ability to get opposing sides of the rangeland conflict to talk to one another. (The Hatfields were instrumental in putting together a collaborative group named the Trout Creek Mountain Group that helped heal the habitat of an endangered fish, the Lahontan cutthroat trout.)

Even though Marston's main interest in the Hatfields was their skill in conflict resolution, he learned that anyone who spends much time around them gets to hear about the land, and how important it is to them. On one of those occasions when Doc was recounting that he had learned how some rangeland plants can perform functions that enable damaged land to once again be home to its natives, Marston said he experienced "an epiphany."

That awakening came as Marston watched Doc kneel and explain how the roots of sagebrush plants could pierce the hardpan created by repeated plowing of land that had been farmed, and how he could manage his animals to graze the land in a way that enabled

When Doc was recounting that he had learned how some rangeland plants can perform functions that enable damaged land to once again be home to its natives, Marston said he experienced "an epiphany."

native plants to take advantage of this phenomenon and recolonize the area. Marston recalled that, as he watched, "It came to me that you couldn't have a vital landscape without a vital human presence on it.

"That experience," Marston continued, "changed the way I look at people and their relationship to the land."

The Hatfields manage the land in this restorative way in order to produce health—healthy food and healthy land.

Ultimately, they believe, this produces a healthy environment, healthy families, and healthy communities, which they will tell you are all one thing.

The Hatfields manage the land in this restorative way in order to produce health—healthy food and healthy land.

THE ADVANTAGES OF USING MORE LAND

One of the greatest claims to fame of technological agriculture is that it uses less land to produce more food. Even Leave-It-Alone environmentalists tout this as a boon. They argue that, because we need less and less land to produce the food we need, we can afford to leave more and more land alone. Doc and Connie, and the other ranchers of OCB, show us this may not be a good thing. Using less and less land to produce food may not be good because producing food the way the Hatfields and others of the new Gardeners of Eden do it produces a lot more than just food. It produces land that absorbs water more effectively and stores it within living systems and makes it available to those systems in a way life can use it. It nurtures and sustains soil microorganisms that make the soil more fertile and more hospitable to seed germination and plant growth. It creates a plant community that is more able to remove carbon from the air and sequester it in stems and roots and the subsurface soil community, thus fighting global warming. Via all of the above, it enables ecosystems to nurture diverse and sustainable communities of wildlife, which help sustain the relationships I've just described.

But producing food on the land produces something that may be more important than all those things I just listed. It produces connection—direct connection in the form of feedback.

Food was the feedback connection between those earlier Gardeners and the land. It is the heart of most mutualistic relationships in nature (if not all of them). Food connects us to the environment in a way that morals can't, that politics can't, that emotions can't. Food is objective, not subjective. You can see it. You can taste it. You can tell when you've got it, and when you haven't. Producing food in the way that Doc and Connie Hatfield produce it, and the way those earlier Gardeners produced it, provides a connection to the land that is direct and verifiable. Perhaps most valuable of all, it makes us aware of what "a direct and verifiable connection to the land" is.

Our modern technologically based agriculture was created to be as disconnected as possible from the environment, to be immune to it. In fact, our food-production technology produces its own environment—its own rainfall (irrigation), its own fertilizer (chemical fertilizer), its own "herd animals" (tractors that churn the ground and inoculate it with fertilizer, the way animals like bison once did). It eliminates competition from other plant and animal species via pesticides. It even produces its own species, via genetic engineering, that are resistant to the feedback functions of nature—insects, diseases, drought, et cetera.

While the Gardeners of Eden were connected to the health of the environment by their need for food and fiber, and by the feedback connections their need for those things sustained, our modern society's means of producing those same necessities disconnects us from the environment.

This has its good side. It means more of us than ever before are able to eat. That's good because there are more of us than ever before who want to eat. It is also good for subscribers to the Leave-It-Alone definition of environmental health because it means we need less land to produce what we need, and we can leave more land alone than we ever could before.

But it has its bad side, too. When our culture began developing an agriculture that required fewer of us to work at producing food, few of us realized we were losing anything. After all, the fact that less of us had to work to produce food meant more of us were free to engage in other activities—commerce, art, science, innovation, leisure. The fact that our environmental philosophy told us (in the myth of the Garden of Eden and elsewhere) that humans could only do damage to nature anyway made it easy to conclude that we weren't only doing ourselves a favor, we were doing nature a favor as well.

As we raised more of our crops and livestock on fields instead of ecosystems, and as hunting became a sport rather than a form of herding, our old feedback loops began to shrivel. As we reduced our vested interest in the health of the ecosystems beyond our fields by ceasing to harvest food from them, we also cut our feedback connections with those ecosystems' ability to perform other ecological functions, such as cycling carbon and capturing and storing water. And we began to call this land "nature." Evidence suggests that we didn't use the word "nature," at least in the sense of something separate from us, until this transformation occurred. Before it happened, there was no "natural/artificial" distinction between us and our surroundings—we were one. By creating the bubble, we created nature,

Food connects us to the environment in a way that morals can't, that politics can't, that emotions can't.

and by doing so we made our gradual metamorphosis into aliens in our own house, our own garden, inevitable.

As we transformed the land outside our bubble into the cathedral, art exhibit, zoo, and adventure park that we consider nature to be, more and more of us declared using this land off-limits because that would be inappropriate in any of the above. We declared inappropriate any activity that would make the landscape appear to be altered and thus sully the art of nature on exhibit there. We declared the animals "wild" and deemed it inappropriate to harvest them by herding them and to use them as tools to manipulate the landscape (as the Gardeners of Eden had done), because that sort of activity would taint the image of nature as wild.

And how can you have an adventure park in a garden?

As for the land's function as a water sequesterer and such, the Leave-It-Alone approach would have us believe that if we just left the land alone, or returned it to what it was before we got here and then left it alone, the land would resume these functions automatically, and it would perform them to the maximum degree ecologically possible. When that didn't happen, as it hasn't in the case of some of the left-alone areas I described earlier, the answer has been the standard one—that humans have disrupted ecological processes so much that the land will take a long time to recover, or that it may never recover.

There we might have remained had not the work of people like Mann, Nabhan, and Margolin revealed to us that humans had played a positive role in the creation of the Edens that existed before there was a bubble, and before we had begun to abandon the Garden. There we might have remained, too, had not the Hatfields, Joe Morris, and other producers of healthy food showed us how we can reconnect these feedback loops without having to go hungry and cold, and how we can do it in the context of a modern society.

There's an added upside to what those renewers of our feedback connections are doing. As more and more of our food is produced by industrial agriculture, more and more of us realize we don't want to eat food produced by an industry. As a result, the production of healthful food on open space is expanding. In addition to natural beef, you can now buy organic beef, grass-fed, and grass-finished beef. You can buy free-range turkey, goats, and lamb, and free-range eggs.

A recent *USA Today* article reports that the market for red meat sold in natural-food stores is estimated at about $300 million to $350 million. In her 2004 book, *Pasture Perfect*, Jo Robinson writes: "There may be more than 1,000 grass-based producers [of animals for food] in the United States and Canada, and still the demand exceeds the supply." (Remember, in one year the membership of Oregon Country Beef expanded from forty to seventy ranches.)

Organic meat, according to USDA standards, must come from animals that have not been given growth hormones, antibiotics, or feed containing animal products. They must have access to organic pastures, and any hay and grain they consume must be organic.

Grass-fed beef has been getting a lot of press lately. The main reason for this is that its health claims go considerably further than the claims for beef designated as "organic" and "natural." The latter two designations are defined in terms of what they don't contain—no pesticides, no hormones, no animal byproducts. Although this negative can be positive for your health, grass-fed beef has been shown to have significant positive features of its own.

As we reduced our vested interest in the health of the ecosystems beyond our fields by ceasing to harvest food from them, we also cut our feedback connections with those ecosystems' ability to perform other ecological functions, such as cycling carbon and capturing and storing water. And we began to call this land "nature."

Grass-fed beef is higher in a number of nutrients, including vitamin E and antioxidants of the carotenoid family, e.g. beta carotene, than meat from animals fattened in feedlots.

Grass-fed beef is two to ten times higher in Omega-3 fatty acids than meat from grain-fed or feedlot animals; in fact, it is nearly as high in Omega-3s as the meat from wild animals—wild bison, for instance. If that bison is fattened in a feedlot, as many are today, it has fewer Omega-3s and more overall fat than a grass-fed cow. Meat from a grass-fed cow even has more Omega-3s and less overall fat than chicken breast. It is also high in another good fatty acid—conjugated linoleic acid (CLA). CLA is relatively new on the health-food scene, having been shown to fight cancer and cardiovascular disease in lab animals. It is produced only by ruminants—animals with multiple stomachs like cattle, sheep, goats, and bison.

The reason more people don't market grass-fed or grass-finished beef is because the benefits of this method of raising animals only occur while the animal is eating grass that's green. The only way to sell grass-fed meat when the grass isn't green is by processing and freezing it while the grass is green, and frozen beef doesn't sell as well as fresh beef. That's why producers who have deals to provide fresh meat year-round, as Oregon Country Beef does, haven't switched to grass-only production.

As the demand grows for more animals produced on pasture, the economic support for keeping land in pasture (in other words, open space) grows as well. The Hatfields and other producers of healthful meats have given us an economic means to support open space to add to the means that already exist.

At present, much of the money that sustains open space comes from land trusts and environmental groups, and from the government. The federal government pays to sustain and maintain millions of acres of open space in the form of national parks and monuments, Forest Service and Bureau of Land Management lands, military reservations, Indian reservations, and so forth. To a lesser but still significant degree, state governments support open space in similar ways. So do land trusts.

Economic support also comes to open space for the roles it plays as cathedral, art gallery, adventure park, and so forth. We spend money to sustain open-space lands by camping on them, hiking over them, birdwatching on them, and joyriding across them. This money creates a vested interest in open space for the people plugged into these cash-flow streams—for equipment sellers, outfitters, concessionaires, government employees, hotel owners, travel magazine publishers, and so forth.

There's another economy that involves open space that most of us don't think about or aren't aware of. That is the conflict economy. In fact, conflict may now be one of the most valuable products, in monetary terms, produced on open space, especially the public lands variety. Conflict may be worth more in dollars than the wood, food, minerals, or ski trips those lands produce. We literally spend billions of dollars fighting over these lands. We send our contributions to groups that use those dollars to initiate a whole list of political and legal

Grass-fed beef is two to ten times higher in Omega-3 fatty acids than meat from grain-fed or feedlot animals; in fact, it is nearly as high in Omega-3s as the meat from wild animals—wild bison, for instance.

actions regarding them. We send money to politicians who run on a platform of winning "the battle for public lands" and who promise to "protect the environment" by removing human impacts from it.

Although the conflict economy represents a vested interest in the existence of open space (if it didn't exist, we wouldn't be able to fight over it), it does little to create or sustain the health of these lands. In fact, it may do more harm than good. In the case of private land, it may even be the most effective means of destroying open space.

When groups bring regulatory or legal action against a landowner, including the government, that landowner has to spend some of his, her, or its budget to respond to that action. Because the budgets of all these players are limited, that means less money is available to improve the land or to change management that has proved harmful or to adopt some of the restorative practices of the new Gardeners of Eden. In the case of private lands, this increase in overhead is proving sufficient to convince a number of landowners to try some other means of or some other place for making a living.

The end result of this is a net loss of the very open space, wildlands, and remote habitat those regulatory or legal actions are supposed to protect. I know this because I've driven the roads around the West and seen the For Sale signs on more ranches than I care to count, and therefore on more open space than I want to contemplate. I know it because I've had rangeland transects I've been monitoring become somebody's yard when the ranch was subdivided.

If you doubt what I'm saying, take a drive through the West and check for yourself.

There are a lot of reasons people sell their ranches and farms. The overhead of conflict in money and stomach acid is just one of those, but the bottom-line reason those ranches aren't bought by other ranchers, and become developments instead, is because there's not enough economic support to keep them as ranches.

The Hatfields and other marketers of natural, organic, grass-fed, and pasture-raised beef have broadened the base of support for open space. Made it more solid. Given more of us a vested interest in keeping it from being

PHOTO: DAN DAGGET

The end result of this is a net loss of the very open space, wildlands, and remote habitat those regulatory or legal actions are supposed to protect.

paved and subdivided. There is another advantage to what they have done. An economy based on the positive values open space can provide for us isn't dependent on villainizing anyone or turning one part of our society against the other, as conflict is.

Even if the demand for healthful, pasture-raised food grows phenomenally, however, it can't create an economy large enough to sustain enough open space to produce the amounts of clean air, clean water, carbon sequestration, and undeveloped land many of us believe the world is going to need. Others have realized this, too, and some of them have taken steps to expand the open-space economy beyond food to include the other products of our mutualistic relationship with animals and the land. Ironically, some of these steps employ an alien means—space-age technology—to enable us to act more like natives. ■

Deseret Ranch, Woodruff, Utah

CHAPTER TEN

BUILDING A NEW ECONOMY FOR EDEN

MARKETING THE FRUITS OF EDEN ▪ YOU CAN'T SELL IT UNLESS YOU
CAN MEASURE IT ▪ THE THREE D'S ▪ ULTRALIGHTS, QUADS, AND IPACS
COWBOYING FROM SATELLITE ▪ TOOL-USING PLANTS
REINTRODUCING OURSELVES TO NATURE

Marketing the ephemeral products of rangeland management, such as carbon and water sequestration, is no easy task. In order to sell them, you have to first be able to prove that you produced them. And then you have to be able to show how much of them you produced. Add to this the fact that what you're trying to sell are small amounts of these values spread over huge expanses of extremely remote land, and you begin to get a picture of the difficulty involved. Toss in the fact that almost nobody believes you can produce these values in the first place, and the challenge starts to rank right up there with the impossible.

Gregg Simonds, a professional ranch manager and consultant from Park City, Utah, has come to be known as one of the most creative marketers of the other products of rangeland management. If anyone is up to this task, people who know Simonds say he's the one.

Simonds established his reputation as a marketer of the other fruits of rangeland management in the late 1970s on the Deseret Ranch in northern Utah. When Simonds came to the Deseret and brought his practice of restorative grazing, he quickly realized that these methods were producing a lot more than just beef. In fact, they were producing a number of things that were of value to people who didn't care a hoot about beef—great wildlife habitat, for instance.

Simonds believes that, if you produce something that other people value, you should be rewarded for it. He believes this because he knows that anyone who is rewarded for producing something will probably produce more of it. Gregg was convinced that, if the Deseret could find a way to be rewarded for enhancing wildlife habitat, it would not only be good for the ranch because it would make it more profitable, it would also be good for the wildlife that used that habitat and for the people who value that wildlife.

Following that line of thought, Simonds put together a wildlife program that was as much a part of the management and sustainability of the ranch as was raising cattle. He hired biologists and made them as much a part of the ranch's management as cowboys. Under this program, which has been continued by ranch manager Bill Hopkin and wildlife manager Rick Danvir, the Deseret's wildlife has prospered. One of the fruits of Simonds' success to first catch broad attention was the Deseret's elk herd. The Deseret has come to be known around the world for its plentiful numbers of these statuesque animals and the size of its bulls. A premium elk hunt on the Deseret costs as much as $12,500, and hunters have to be selected by lottery.

Other animals of interest to hunters, such as mule deer and pronghorn, have prospered under the Deseret's management, too, but the ranch's success hasn't been limited to huntable species.

Other animals of interest to hunters, such as mule deer and pronghorn, have prospered under the Deseret's management, too, but the ranch's success hasn't been limited to huntable species. The lands of the ranch, which encompass an exceptionally broad variety of habitats, from desert shrublands to montane forests, have also come to be known as among the best places in North America to go bird-watching. Mark Stackhouse of Westwings Tours, which leads bird-watching outings on the ranch, has observed 272 species there. Of these, Stackhouse says, 155 are known to breed within the ranch's boundaries. As I mentioned earlier, the Deseret holds the Utah state bird-watching record for the most species seen in a single day. On the ranch, reaching the bird-watching benchmark of sighting a hundred species in a single day is a regular occurrence. In fact, Mark says, "It's hard not to see at least a hundred if you're out for a whole day." One tour group Stackhouse took to the ranch saw 50 species from the window of the guesthouse on a single spring day when an unanticipated snowstorm kept them inside.

Endangered species? The Deseret has gained a reputation as a haven for them, too. Take sage grouse, for instance. Sage grouse are a candidate for the Threatened and Endangered list. With 20 percent of the sagebrush habitat in Utah's Ridge County, the Deseret is home to 80 percent of the county's sage grouse. That's according to information from the Utah Division of Wildlife Resources. Going back to Mark Stackhouse again, Mark says, "Twenty-five years ago, the ranch had 600 [sage] grouse. Now it has 2,500. I don't know of any other place that had a significant population that has experienced that kind of increase."

Most of the economic payoff the Deseret has received for these successes has come in the enhancement of the ranch's reputation as a good steward of wildlife and the environment. This has reduced the amount of lawsuits and other items of conflict "overhead" it has to face. In these days when conflict marketers can make more off a rancher's land than the rancher, that is no small consideration.

But even good stewards get sued these days. When I visited the Deseret recently, Bill Hopkin told me that the ranch, along with its neighbors, had been made the target of a lawsuit by a group infamous for its ability to ply the conflict economy.

"They've actually done us a favor," Hopkin told me. "I don't think anything would have been as effective at getting us and our neighbors together as that lawsuit has been."

While Simonds was successfully developing a program for marketing the wildlife values produced by the Deseret, he was brainstorming ways to market other values the restorative management of the ranch was producing. Simonds felt these values, which I've called ephemeral, could be more valuable than wildlife, and even beef, in the long run. The first of these values he set out to market was the capacity of the ranch to capture, clean, and store water. Few things could be more important to the West's increasingly urban and thirsty society. Simonds was confident the ranch's lub-dub grazing program was increasing its ability to capture water and store it in its ecosystems, releasing it slowly via clear-running springs rather than sediment-laden flash floods. He was confident of this because the grass on the ranch stayed green longer since the management had changed; the springs and streams on the ranch ran longer; and there were more critters out there—more bugs, more birds, more moose, and more sound. The ranch buzzed and tweeted more than it had before.

With Salt Lake City at the base of the mountain, with headline after headline trumpeting a growing western water crisis, with new dams too environmentally hot to handle and existing dams storing less water and more silt than anyone thought they would, Simonds grew more and more convinced that there had to be a way to market the ranch's ability to store water in ecosystems rather than reservoirs. As time went on, this awareness extended to other values the ranch was producing that were also in demand—carbon sequestration, critical habitat for endangered species, a way to fight the invasion of noxious weeds.

For a long time Simonds did what a lot of other ranchers do. He wrote off the money he put into improving management as part of the overhead of beef production. Simonds had made the Deseret one of the most profitable ranches in the West, and the fact that it was able to produce beef as efficiently as it did no doubt had something to do with the fact that it stored water and sequestered carbon as effectively as it did. In a way, therefore, it made sense to write these expenses off as beef expenses. But there were better reasons not to. Since Simonds knew that, if the ranch was rewarded directly for producing values such as water storage, it would produce a lot more of them, and he knew that being rewarded for doing so could make the ranch a lot more solid economically, eventually, he believed, these other values could become the ranch's main source of sustainability. In that case, beef would become a byproduct, and the ranch and its open space could remain in business for a long, long time.

In order for this to happen, however, he knew he would have to come up with a way to market these values on their own and not just as value-added aspects of the beef the ranch produced.

"I want to get it [the market in "other" values] to work on its own," Simonds explained, "so you won't need to put on dog-and-pony shows at the ranch."

Other ranchers—the ranchers of Oregon Country Beef, for example—use ranch tours, Grazewell Principles, meet-the-ranch-family days, and other forms of what Simonds calls dog-and-pony shows to prove that they're taking good care of the land. Simonds's aim was to take these interchanges out of the subjective realm of show-and-tell and put them into the objective realm of direct commerce, like buying a car. When you buy a car, you don't have to have someone convince you that you bought one—you take the keys, get in, and drive away.

Simonds grew more and more convinced that there had to be a way to market the ranch's ability to store water in ecosystems rather than reservoirs.

Simonds has reduced this more direct way of marketing to what he calls the three D's—principles he believes are required to market anything to anybody.

The first of the three D's stands for "Define." In this case, defining something means being able to identify it, being able to point to it and say, "I'll sell you X amount of that." This also requires being able to measure whatever you're selling.

"Until you can measure something," explains Simonds, "you can't get paid for it."

The two other D's stand for "Defend" and "Divest." To defend something means being able to defend your claim that you are a supplier of whatever it is, that you can produce it and deliver it. Or you can choose to not deliver it. You can't charge people for rain because you can't make it rain or not rain, but you can charge them for delivering rain in the form of water that comes out of their faucet.

Divest means you have to be able to deliver something in such a way that the receiver recognizes that you have delivered it, that they can take ownership of it, and that they can use it or gain advantage from it.

For some things, the three D's are easy. Take, for instance, those big bull elk on the Deseret. If you want one, you have to go to the Deseret to get it. And you can't do that unless you're lucky enough to get drawn in the lottery, and you pay your fee.

Measuring the amount of carbon that a particular management approach has caused to be sequestered on a large piece of rangeland is an undertaking of mind-boggling complexity.

Not so with something like carbon sequestration. Take the first D. Measuring the amount of carbon that a particular management approach has caused to be sequestered on a large piece of rangeland is an undertaking of mind-boggling complexity. First of all, the natural variation across rangelands in the West is immense. Some areas have almost no plants at all and therefore sequester almost no carbon. Other areas have stands of perennial grasses that comprise significant biomass and therefore sequester significant amounts of carbon. How significant? Remember Pete Jackson's statement about how a healthy grassland is more effective at removing carbon from the air (by sequestering it) than an acre of rainforest.

Because variations are large and the areas being monitored are huge, costs to measure these values can be astronomical. Using technology, however, Simonds has been able to get these costs down to pennies an acre; 7.5 cents an acre on one ranch, he claims. To do this, he uses computers, satellites, ultralight airplanes, hand-held computer devices, remote electronic monitoring devices…The list continues to grow.

Simonds described how he molds all this sophisticated technology into an economic monitoring system as he, Tom Bean, and I sat around a coffee table in the lobby of a hotel in Park City, Utah. As I watched and Tom photographed, Simonds spread a large map out on the table and began pointing at its various features and describing how they were arrived at. The document was glossy and colorful, like a map produced to illustrate the rise in temperature of the oceans, the drying of the Gobi Desert, the extent of Alexander the Great's advance. This was obviously a sales device and an educational tool as well as a monitoring implement.

"We start with soil maps because the potential of an area comes from its soil," Simonds explained. "Then we get vegetation maps and start combining them. The vegetation maps are federal maps, but they have big inaccuracies. So we get guys with four-wheelers and digital cameras, GPS devices, and iPAC pocket computers and send them out to correct the maps."

As l watched and Tom photographed, Simonds spread a large map out on the table and began pointing at its various features and describing how they were arrived at

The four-wheeler crews collect digital photos and monitoring data from a variety of locations and, where they find the vegetative map to be wrong, they enter the correct data. Computers then extrapolate the data to other areas with the same characteristics.

"After a while, we start getting a lot more detail and the map starts getting a lot more accurate," Simonds continued.

When the map seems to have become fairly accurate, the monitoring crew uses an airplane to do broader checks, followed by more ground-truthing and additional map detailing. At some point, the map-checking starts to become redundant, the ground-truthers start finding what the map tells them they will find, and the map becomes accurate enough to be used as a management tool. "Basically, we use it to locate problems and potentials," Simonds said. "Then we use grazing and other practices to solve those problems and actuate the potentials."

Simonds' high-tech feedback connections with the land don't stop there. He uses in-stream monitoring devices to measure flow rates and levels of turbidity to define the degree to which his management increases the ranch's ability to store water, clean it, and release it more evenly over time. To monitor the health of streamside habitats for grants involving endangered species, Simonds has hired a pilot to fly an ultralight airplane 40 mph a hundred feet off the ground taking digital photos at short time intervals for the length of the stream. This, supplemented with more ground-truthing and extrapolation, can give an accurate picture of a stream's habitat value.

The map enables Simonds to extrapolate information gathered in this way over the entire ranch. For instance, once carbon sequestration rates have been determined for a certain kind of grassland under a certain kind of management, the map enables Simonds to give an accurate estimation of how much carbon is being (or can be) sequestered by that habitat type over the whole ranch. The same goes for water sequestration and other values.

This type of monitoring can supply accurate information on how much of the ranch can be altered or used as-is to provide habitat for an endangered species to mitigate the loss of that habitat elsewhere. It can also reveal areas on the ranch that may already support a species of interest for its TES status or any of a number of other reasons.

Divesting these values is more of a challenge. Some of the nontypical values ranches produce have a marketplace in which they are traded. Some don't. For the most part, trading in these values is in the startup phase. According to Simonds, the fact that the U.S. has not signed the Kyoto Accord regarding global warming stands as an obstacle to developing large-scale marketing of carbon sequestration here, in the world's largest producer of atmospheric carbon. Had the U.S. signed the agreement, Simonds wouldn't have time to talk to me about how to do this; he would be too busy doing it.

Although startup is slower than it would be under the Kyoto Treaty, the marketing of these values in the U.S. is growing. So is talk of how it can benefit agriculture.

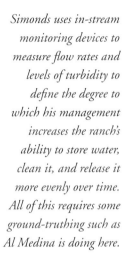

Simonds uses in-stream monitoring devices to measure flow rates and levels of turbidity to define the degree to which his management increases the ranch's ability to store water, clean it, and release it more evenly over time. All of this requires some ground-truthing such as Al Medina is doing here.

"I've seen where carbon sequestration has sold for about $25 a ton," says Simonds. "A ranch, even in this dry country, can sequester about a ton of carbon per acre. Twenty-five dollars an acre, that's a very good return for a rancher in this kind of country."

The same sophisticated technologies that can be used to help producers market those hard-to-market values can help produce them as well. On one 100,000-acre ranch Simonds is managing, he is in the process of installing an extensive livestock-watering system that can be controlled electronically.

"Those eighty troughs give us eighty pastures," he explains, pointing out that the watering system can be used to control cattle almost as effectively as fences and to move them almost as effectively as cowboys. If Simonds concludes that he wants to graze one part of the ranch "to solve some problem or achieve some potential," he can "just turn the water off on the part of the ranch we want the cows to leave, and turn it on where we want them to go."

If Simonds concludes that he wants to graze one part of the ranch "to solve some problem or achieve some potential," he can "just turn the water off on the part of the ranch we want the cows to leave, and turn it on where we want them to go."

Using this method, Simonds can use his cattle to tackle some of the most pressing environmental problems facing the West today. One of those most pressing problems is the rapid spread of one of the West's most aggressive invaders—cheatgrass or downy brome (Bromus tectorum).

Cheatgrass is a wispy annual that produces little in the way of carbon sequestration or forage for wildlife or livestock. It has become the dominant herbaceous plant on about twenty-five million acres of the West and is expanding those holdings rapidly. In many of the areas it has invaded, it has become a virtual monoculture. Its effectiveness as an invader is enhanced by a characteristic it has that we usually don't associate with a plant: It is a tool-user, and a very accomplished one at that. The tool it uses is fire. A number of plants use fire to trigger their seeds to germinate under the right conditions. Some use fire as cheatgrass does—to eliminate competitors and invade and secure territory.

Cheatgrass completes its growth cycle, goes to seed, and turns into waving seas of flammable tinder just at the time the West is most prone to fire—when summer lightning storms and vacationers' campfires and cigarettes are most common. As a result of this opportunism, areas with a high cheatgrass content burn frequently. In fact, one of the ways Simonds identifies areas he suspects of being invaded by cheatgrass is by checking how frequently they have burned.

This affinity for fire is good for cheatgrass and bad for its competitors because cheatgrass is able to withstand fire better than most other plants—certainly better than native perennials. Unlike those perennials, what little carbon cheatgrass sequesters is pumped into the air with disturbing regularity as smoke rather than into the soil.

"Spread over millions of acres, imagine how much carbon this has contributed to global warming," Simonds challenged.

Since cheatgrass is an annual plant, its growth cycle can be interrupted by grazing. If it is grazed before it goes to seed, it won't grow back as a perennial would. It has to wait till the next season to grow from seed. If this happens a number of years in a row, it can seriously interrupt the plant's invasive cycle. This control-by-eating has been done a number of times in a number of cases, so we know it works at least to a degree, and with repeated applications it works even better.

The conventional means to deal with this aggressive invader is to spray it with an herbicide. Evidence indicates, however, that cheatgrass is especially adapted to grow in areas where the soil is deficient of microflora and microfauna. Spraying herbicides on a piece of land invaded by cheatgrass further diminishes the land's soil microbial community and makes it even more hospitable to the invader—sort of like Brer Fox tossing Brer Rabbit into that briar patch. Using animals to fight cheatgrass has the opposite effect. Grazing in a lub-dub way pumps carbon and organic material into the soil, providing nutrition to support the regrowth of a healthy and diverse microbial community. That makes the land less hospitable for cheatgrass and more hospitable to more desirable perennials, just as Elaine Ingham of Soil Food Web, Inc., has told us it would.

Since satellites can monitor for greenness, Simonds can use his technology to tell him when and where the cheatgrass is green and growing and most vulnerable to having its annual cycle interrupted by grazing. Then he can use the watering system to put the animals where he needs them. Finally, the map can be used to indicate the extent of this success and to identify areas where it can be expanded.

Although Simonds's approach is definitely space-age, it is nonetheless a reincarnation of the methods of the Gardeners of the pre-Columbian Eden. In a very significant way, it

Grazing and fire have been used to cause native perennial grasses and other beneficial species to replace cheat-grass and other invaders on this rangeland on the Deseret Ranch in Utah.

may be one of the most accurate reincarnations we have today because Simonds' method uses feedback the same way those ancient Gardeners did. He measures success in terms of results on the land, as the Gardeners did. He doesn't measure it in terms of how the land is managed, as our contemporary alien environmentalism does.

When the Gardeners' relationship with nature didn't work, when what they were doing didn't produce the results they intended, they went hungry and cold. That kind of feedback is easy to read. It's direct and objective. Not many would argue its accuracy.

Same for Simonds' approach. When he doesn't get the results he says he can, he doesn't get paid. If he fails, he doesn't get an "E" for effort or a consolation prize for doing the right thing. He gets paid for results. No results, no pay. That's pretty simple, too. And if he blames his failure on someone else (the guys that had that land before I did messed it up so bad it'll never produce), he still doesn't get paid. ■

CHAPTER ELEVEN

BECOMING NATIVE AGAIN— TOWARD A NEW ENVIRONMENTALISM

GONE PACK HUNTING LATELY? ▪ A COLLEGE COURSE ON EDEN

DISCOVERING THE VALUE OF EARLIER CULTURES

A UNIFIED ENVIRONMENTAL THEORY ▪ REVOKING THE FREE

PASS FOR THE LEAVE-IT-ALONE ASSUMPTION

For those of us who value becoming more native and less alien and who are interested in reestablishing the same sort of connection with nature that the earlier Gardeners of Eden had, Gregg Simonds' methods are extremely valuable. They're valuable because most of us can't directly participate in the kind of mutualisms the earlier Gardeners used and Lost Tribers continue to use. Most of us don't have a ranch and a bunch of animals we can go herding across the landscape, nor do we have a big piece of land on which we are free to build trincheras and rock dams. And even if we tried pursuing herds of animals, we'd be stopped by suburbs, freeways, golf courses, and shopping centers. (I sometimes fantasize about driving a herd of cattle across a golf course—to restore it, you know.) If we tried to hunt in packs we'd run afoul of the game laws. Start a fire?!!! You'd better be ready to do serious prison time.

While it's true that we can remain connected to the land via the feedback relationships provided by healthful food of the sort that the Hatfields and the Morrises produce, the kind of environmental values that Gregg Simonds produces provide an even more direct way of doing so. Most of us aren't in a position to directly purchase those values, but we can influence the entities that do—governments, NGOs, and corporations. Because a lot of the obstacles the marketing of these values faces are legislative and regulative, we can support them in the conventional way—by writing our representatives in Congress and participating in the land-management planning process and such. If all that sounds unexciting for you (I've never been all that excited about writing my congressman), there are more stimulating things you can do.

One of those more stimulating things was revealed to me while I was giving a presentation at one of the Bioneers' annual international environmental conferences in Marin, California. It happened just after I asked my audience if any of them had taken care of their environmental responsibilities that day: Had any of them gone hunting in a pack? Started any grass fires? Piled rocks in any gullies? Chased any bison off a cliff?

At that, a few people jumped up and ran out. I wasn't surprised. I didn't think there would be a lot of herd hunters in attendance. Those who remained listened to me tell about the positive roles humans have played in the environment—a shorter version of what I've just told you. After they heard me out, a couple of them came up with the idea that someone should create a college-level program to study the roles humans have played as a part of nature and teach other people about them. It seemed like a great idea to me, and I told them so. As far as I know, such programs are rare. Examples are limited to schools of hard knocks and applied science such as Learning-on-the-Fringe U. at Mina, Nevada, and emerging programs such as the Center for Sustainable Environments at Northern Arizona University in Flagstaff, a program headed by ethnoecologist Gary Nabhan. Expanding this area of study and research to more mainstream institutions with more resources would, without doubt, make the idea that humans have been an important part of nature a lot more respectable, credible, and more broadly accepted.

The fact that there is no organized course of study in this topic should come as no surprise in light of the widespread acceptance of the Leave-It-Alone assumption. The good news here is that this lack means the field of study is wide open, and what a field it is! Who

Everett Sparling performing the predator function, herding cattle with his dogs near San Juan Bautista, California.

wouldn't love to discover how important we are to nature, and how we can restore nature to some kind of functioning harmony that includes us. That seems so much more rewarding than trying to fool her into thinking we were never here or, worse yet, withdrawing to our space-station-like techno-bubbles.

Another advantage to expanding this area of study is that it would teach us some things that we might otherwise never know about the value of the earlier Gardeners of Eden, the people we now call American Indians or Native Americans, or whom we know by different names in other parts of the world. Learning these things would increase our appreciation of those people immensely. Right now, we value earlier peoples for a lot of things—for their values and their culture, for their bravery and resourcefulness in war, for their spiritual connection to nature, for their dances and ceremonies, for the dramatic and colorful nature of their adornment. But when it comes to how they managed the environment, the thing most of us value about those peoples is the perception that there were so few of them they couldn't really mess things up. In other words, we value them for being a failure, because that's what most of us assume they were.

The stories you've read here should convince you that the opposite is true. The stories told by Margolin and Pyne establish that the earlier Gardeners didn't just impact the environment, they shaped it. In some instances they created it. By so doing, they weren't a failure. They were a success—in some cases an unsurpassed success. Those successes deserve to be studied, not as primitive curiosities, but as examples of effective management worthy of understanding and emulation. Contemporary members of the Gardeners of Eden already understand this and are taking advantage of it.

Before you get too involved in emulating those earlier Gardeners, however, I want to insert an important caveat. Remember our earlier discussion about how practitioners of Leave-It-Alone environmentalism assume that the health of an environment is solely a matter of the process by which it is managed? Specifically, they assume it is a matter of the degree to which that environment is protected. Remember how that led to the absurd conclusion that a habitat that's home to no flycatchers is more valuable than one that hosts the largest known population of them? And the equally absurd conclusion that, if a piece of land is left alone, "even if it becomes as bare as a parking lot," it is more natural, and therefore better, than a piece of land that is stewarded by humans, no matter what its condition?

If we become so taken with learning how the earlier Gardeners managed the land and begin emulating them as enthusiastically as I believe some of us would, we could find ourselves right back in this very same dilemma. We could find ourselves with our feedback loops plugged into what we're doing instead of into how the land is faring.

This would be easy for us to do. We humans are process-oriented animals. (Maybe all animals are.) We think in terms of processes. We learn in terms of processes. If we want to learn how to create a certain result, we watch someone else create it, and then we do what

If we become so taken with learning how the earlier Gardeners managed the land that we begin emulating them, we could find ourselves with our feedback loops plugged into what we're doing instead of into how the land is faring.

he did. In other words, we assume if we do something the same way someone else does it, we'll get the same results. When it comes to the environment, we have altered this a bit—we think that if we do the right thing (manage the environment in the right way), we'll get the right results. This, I believe, is how a lot of us (including me, during the activist part of my environmental career) end up thinking that the health of the environment is a matter of the way it is managed, rather than its condition.

This has got us into trouble before. It got us into trouble when we carved the Great Plains into homesteads because creating a nation of Jeffersonian small farms was the right thing to do. The trouble came when those industrious farmers plowed up the prairie and watched the soil blow away in the dust storms of the Great Depression. Same with the buffalo hunters who killed off the bison because the right thing to do was to tame the wilderness in order to pursue our nation's manifest destiny. That instance of "doing the right thing" had all kinds of negative results, but I'm sure the people who did it were absolutely convinced they were doing the right thing, and no feedback would have convinced them otherwise. If you know you're doing the right thing, you keep doing it even when the grass starts to die, the springs dry up, and the soil blows away. In fact, if you're convinced you're doing the right thing and bad things start to happen, you don't stop; you do it harder.

While it is true that if we wish to live in a mutualistic harmony with nature we would be well advised to learn from the ways of the earlier Gardeners, and even emulate them, we can't assume that just using the methods they used will automatically get the results we want. Times are different. The problems are different. The land is different. What we want is different.

There is one important exception to this. This exception leads us to something that could be called a "Unified Principle of Environmentalism." The unified part comes from the fact that, when you get right down to it, those earlier Gardeners only used one method to get the results they got, the results we now marvel at (at least in some cases). They might have used different tactics to implement that method—they may have hunted by herding, burned the grasslands, dug bulbs with a stick—but there was only one method that produced their success: They tried something and noted the results, and when they got the results they wanted, they continued doing what they were doing. And when they didn't get the results they wanted, they did something different.

Some of you will recognize that as "plan, do, study, act" (PDSA)—one of the core processes of several contemporary effective-management systems. Others will recognize it as a shorthand description of the scientific method. A few will recognize it as one of the core elements of Holistic Management. It is also one of the main principles of conflict resolution, collaborative problem-solving, and team-building.

Still others will recognize it as the essence of life and evolution: Living things adapt. Inanimate objects (and living things destined for evolution's scrap heap) don't. Fritjof Capra, author of *The Tao of Physics* and *The Web of Life: A New Scientific Understanding of Living Systems*, calls this strategy "self-organization" and identifies it as "perhaps the central concept in the systems view of life." By the act of setting a goal, working to achieve it, reading the feedback, and correcting what we do, we act as a living system would act. If this book is to help establish a new environmentalism (as one of the people who reviewed it suggested) this

By the act of setting a goal, working to achieve it, reading the feedback, and correcting what we do, we act as a living system would act.

strategy, which is a cornerstone of management, science, evolution, holism, and life, would be the central strategy of that environmentalism. What could be more appropriate than that?

In order to function, however, this strategy needs goals because the function of feedback is to measure progress toward a goal. And those goals must be concrete in order to avoid plugging our feedback connections into the process by which we manage the land instead of the condition of the land. Those flatworms I mentioned earlier, and the algae that inhabited their guts, they had goals—their own survival and procreation. The bison-hunting, fire-starting Indians of the Great Plains hunted and burned to achieve their goals—the production of what they needed and wanted from those broad grasslands. Because they had goals, they could tell when their methods were working and when they weren't.

Oddly enough, setting concrete goals for natural systems is anathema to our contemporary, alien Leave-It-Alone environmentalism. "Humans don't have the right to set goals for nature," I've been told. "Only nature has that right."

Setting goals of this sort is something we will have to relearn in order to have a functioning feedback connection with nature, a mutualistic connection. That won't be easy for some of us, but we're learning. Mark Thatcher and his wife, Rachel, the people whose commitment to the environment made this book possible, live on a ranch along the central California coast. The land of that ranch is divided among people who bought pieces of it because they wanted to live in relatively undeveloped open space in a beautiful setting. The land between the residences is still operated as a cattle ranch. At first, the residents viewed the cattle with mixed feelings. Because the ranch manager, John McCarty, was doing such a good job of stewarding the land, however, that began to change. Now some residents view the ranching operation as a means to sustain and even restore the

Some people are discovering that, as they live in these beautiful places, they can participate in sustaining and even restoring the ecological health of the land.

ecological health of the land. They're talking about using it to bring back native grasses, restore the health of the riparian areas, revitalize watersheds, and more.

For years while I was living in Flagstaff I worked with a collaborative group named the Diablo Trust that is an example of ranchers and environmentalists who don't live on the ranch working together in this way. That group is still together and still serving as a model of the effectiveness of diverse people working toward shared goals.

Examples of this sort of urban-agri mutualism are cropping up around the West—of people living with or at least working with entities that use the land and produce things from it and contribute to its well-being and their quality of life by doing so. This is another way of placing our relationship with nature on a feedback basis.

Still another way we can do so is by revoking the free pass we have given to the Leave-It-Alone assumption. That would mean holding the Leave-It-Alone approach as environmentally accountable as we now hold all its competitors. We know leaving the land alone has negative impacts. We know from the examples of the desertification of the Drake Exclosure, the difference in water absorption and carbon sequestration capabilities of grazed and rested land on Gene Goven's ranch (remember the honey bear), the examples of sand food, Brodiaea bulbs, Tomales Bay clams, southwestern willow flycatchers, Verde River spikedace, and on and on. What's more, monitoring techniques like those developed by Gregg Simonds, Al Medina, and Jim Richardson now give us a way to verify this and to measure these impacts and extrapolate them over large landscapes. For the first time, this means we can know what the effects of leaving large amounts of the land alone will be. And, because we can apply these same techniques to the effects of managing the land the way Gardeners like Gene Goven and Dave Ogilvie do, we can compare the two methods and decide which is best for us and the environment based on results rather than rhetoric.

We already have the tools it would take to make leaving the land alone accountable. NEPA, the National Environmental Policy Act, requires that the impact of all management activities on public land be assessed and mitigated where those impacts are negative, or some other course of action chosen. Other environmental laws and regulations affecting private as well as public land work in this same way. Those Forest Service staffers on that field trip to the Drake told me that NEPA routinely isn't applied to leaving the land alone because it is assumed to be the absence of use and, therefore, the absence of activities that have negative impacts. We now know that assumption is false. Making current land-management laws and regulations apply to leaving the land alone wouldn't require changing them. It would merely require applying them the way it appears they were intended to be applied—to all activities that significantly affect the environment. How could anyone who considers himself concerned about the environment object to that?

If you're interested in how, as an urbanite, you can become a Gardener by doing something more exciting than writing your congressman, here it is. You can become involved in any of the hundreds, maybe thousands, of NEPA or NEPA-style proceedings that go on every year across the country and work to make leaving the land alone as accountable as any other management method. Actually, a number of the members of the Lost Tribe I have mentioned, and a lot of the ones I haven't, work with teams of interested citizens who do just this sort of thing. Your help would, in most cases, be more than welcome.

At the very least, the next time you pick up a newspaper or some environmental newsletter and read that some place is going to be protected as if that's the end of the matter, as if that will solve all of that place's problems, it is my hope that you find yourself asking, almost without thinking: "Will protecting the land really do what they assume it will do? What results do they intend to achieve by protecting it? Are they going to monitor to see if those results are achieved? What will the negative impacts be and will they do anything to mitigate those negative impacts? If this instance of protection would remove from the land people who are living in a mutualistic relationship with it, I hope you'll ask the same questions, express the same concerns, and offer the same resistance that, in the past, you reserved for actions that threatened predators or endangered species.

If that happens, you will have identified yourself as a native, a member of the Lost Tribe, one of the Gardeners of Eden, and this book will have achieved its purpose. Then we can both celebrate. ■

EPILOGUE

lthough this book has come to an end, the stories it chronicles continue to unfold, and the way of relating to nature it describes—humans acting as natives rather than aliens—remains a matter of awakening and discovery. I was reminded of this in a very direct way, recently, at the fourth annual conference of the Quivira Coalition in Albuquerque, New Mexico. Every year this conference offers to a growing audience presentations based on examples of collaborative stewardship of rangelands similar to the ones I've described in the chapters you've just read. This year's conference (2005) was attended by well over five hundred people. Among those attendees were Democrats and Republicans, preservationists and wise-users, government regulators and anti-regulators, food-close-to-home anti-corporationists and employees of large corporations.

I believe the audience that attends this get-together is one of the most diverse to attend any environmental conference. To me, it serves as a measure of the breadth of the sentiment that, no matter how much we may disagree over environmental issues, we can still find common ground when we think of nature in terms of what we want instead of what we want each other to do.

From Utah State professor Dr. Fred Provenza's mind-expanding talk on his observations that grazing animals have a culture (Provenza described how animals teach one another adaptive strategies such as what to eat in unfamiliar environments), to the banquet made up solely of food raised within 200 miles of the conference—one of the most delicious I have ever enjoyed—the gathering was a resounding success.

Such an event is an exceptional place in which to catch up on what's new among people as widely dispersed as the Lost Tribe, and I did a lot of that. The conference also helped me realize the obvious—that such a catching-up would be the best way to end this book.

At the conference I ran into Doc and Connie Hatfield, who reported that Oregon Country Beef continues to grow and enjoy even greater success. Doc told me that he and Connie are now traveling around the West "replicating" OCB-like co-ops in other areas. Grass-fed beef seems to be growing in popularity, too. I had dinner one night with the Morrises—Joe and his parents Richard and Anne, and Joe talked about the growing demand for this nutritious food. My experience confirms this. It seems like every day I hear about another ranch that has struck up a deal with a local health food market or restaurant to sell grass-fed beef.

The Tiptons didn't attend the conference, but a phone call catch-up afterwards revealed that they are proceeding in typical Tipton-esque fashion. Currently, they are reviving a truck stop that shares its parking lot with the Wildcat Ranch (site of Mina's only ATM). Being Nevadans, and therefore incorrigible prospectors, these most effective land-restorers are confident that this project will finally hit the jackpot for them. Like the true Lost Tribers they are, however, they don't intend to turn their expected good fortune into a condo in Florida or a villa in Southern California. They plan to use the money to provide more funds for their land restoration efforts.

Rain has been plentiful this year in Nevada, as it has been in a lot of areas around the West, and the Tiptons are expecting this year's monitoring to reveal that their restoration efforts are yielding dramatic results. As for the competition, "This year no one will be able to claim that the lands being left alone aren't doing well because it's been too dry," Jerrie declared.

On the Verde River in Arizona, the long-awaited big flood that Leave-It-Alone advocates have contended would bring back the spikedace has happened in spades. After years of drought there were five floods this year, some of which were real gully-washers. Dave Gipe of the Rio Verde Ranch reports that, during one event, streamside gauges reveal that the river rose eight feet in fifteen minutes. The Gipes were alerted to that flood by the sound of trees snapping as they were bulldozed by the wall of water rushing down the canyon. Preliminary reports indicate, however, that the reduction in nonnative predatory fish (small-mouth bass and catfish) expected to accompany such a flood has not happened. Chances that flooding will bring back the spikedace, therefore, are slim, and hope that leaving the river alone will resurrect the endangered fish appears to have faded further. That would seem to enhance the chances for acceptance of the ranchers' proposal to graze part of the river to see if they can recreate the conditions that once sustained the spikedace and, thus, coax it back out of extinction. Supporters of the plan to poison the whole river, however, seem to still hold sway.

Up in North Dakota, Gene Goven reports that a recent study shows that ranchers who employ the type of holistic grazing he uses experience an average return on their money of 16 percent. Practitioners of other approaches, mostly seasonal grazing, report a 2 percent gain. As for the land, "Oh, it just keeps getting better," Goven deadpans with his North Dakota twang. When I told him what I had said about him in the book, Gene reminded me that those aren't his cows that get such good results on his ranch. They belong to someone else who pays to have them grazed on the Goven Ranch. The holistic planning model he uses brought him to the conclusion that he could make more money letting someone else own the cattle as long as he maintained control over how they were managed.

On the U Bar Ranch, southwestern willow flycatchers had another good year. The most recent count there totaled 315 adults, 152 pairs, and 162 territories. The count on the Bennett, the habitat created by David Ogilvie to be flycatcher-friendly, was up—77 adults, 36 pairs, and 41 territories. That makes the Bennett's restored habitat the home of the largest concentration of those endangered birds on the U-Bar, home of the largest population overall.

I'm sure there are other developments by members of the Lost Tribe that are worth reporting that I'm not including here. A group as creative as this is difficult to keep abreast of. So, I'll leave it up to you, with your Leave-It-Alone blinders removed, to keep your eyes open for other reports of successes created by humans acting as natives rather than aliens.

To add heart to your search, I would like to end with a story that harks back to the situation that helped inspire me to write this book—the situation which, in the introduction, I compared to showing dog photos to cat fanatics. You remember—I was showing my slides to those Leave-It-Alone advocates, and they were giving me those, "Don't call us, We'll call you" looks.

Just before this book went to the proofreader, I gave a presentation to the Sierra Nevada Deep Ecology Institute (SNDEI—pronounced Cindy) in Nevada City, California. As I prepared for that presentation, I wondered how my message would fare with this audience. Would it achieve the goal I wrote this book to achieve? Would the role of humans as Gardeners be accepted as a valid alternative to the Leave-It-Alone assumption? This group was certainly familiar with that assumption. Or would the message meet resistance, even hostility? Certain aspects of this book are, after all, quite critical of contemporary environmentalism's bedrock beliefs.

I need not to have worried. The story of the Gardeners was received with warmth and enthusiasm. People said it presented nature in a light they had never thought of. Marge Kaiser, the founder of SNDEI reported, "Everyone loved your talk and the board was very pleased with the event overall and the connections we made to the ranching community as a result." The most interesting response, however, came from Marge herself.

"The other day, as I was driving down the wooded road near my home in the Sierra Foothills," she wrote in an e-mail later, "I started thinking about the subtitle of your book, *Rediscovering Our Importance 'to' Nature*. I looked at the trees and asked, 'Am I really important to you?' Suddenly I felt, emanating from the trees and the whole surround, a reverberating YES!! At that moment, I stepped into nature, in the heart of the web. Tears formed in my eyes. This was a very different world." ■

Dan Dagget is an author, public speaker, and a consultant on collaborative conflict resolution and restorative land management. His first book, *Beyond the Rangeland Conflict, Toward a West That Works* was nominated for a Pulitzer Prize and has been recognized as one of the most important books recently written about environmental issues in the American West. Of that book Wendell Berry wrote: "I read this book eagerly, recognizing it as something I have been waiting for, and it gave me hope...."

Dagget's work is directed toward bridging the gap between environmentalists and rural agriculturists in the American West. For 32 years he has been involved as an activist with a number of environmental groups, from Earth First! to Audubon. In 1992 he was named one of the top 100 grassroots activists in America by the Sierra Club for their John Muir Centennial Celebration. Since the publication of his first book, he has given presentations on the topics of ecosystem restoration and environmental conflict resolution in venues across the West to audiences ranging from activist vegetarians to associations of ranchers and beef producers.

Dagget is the founder of EcoResults! a not-for-profit organization which supports on-the-ground projects to restore damaged ecosystems. He currently lives in Santa Barbara, California, with his wife Trish, but keeps close ties to Flagstaff, Arizona, his adopted hometown.

Tom Bean is a free-lance photographer based in Flagstaff, Arizona. His photographs are seen in hundreds of publications including National Geographic and Smithsonian books. He has a particular interest in creating images that illustrate the positive interactions of culture and the natural world.

Of working on the *Gardeners of Eden,* Tom says: "*Gardeners of Eden* has been an especially exciting opportunity to document encouraging examples of how we can work with natural processes to bring about healthier environments both biologically and economically."